First Edition
Contributing Membership
Smithsonian National Associate Program

A Smithsonian Nature Book

The Great
Gray Owl

Phantom of the Northern Forest

ROBERT W. NERO

Photographs by **ROBERT R. TAYLOR**

Smithsonian Institution Press, Washington, D.C.

Paperback edition 1987

Library of Congress Cataloging in Publication Data
Nero, Robert W.
The great gray owl-phantom of the northern forest.
(A Smithsonian nature book)
Bibliography: p.
Includes index.
Supt. of Docs. no.: SI 1.2:OW4
1. Great gray owl.   2. Birds—Manitoba.   I. Title.
II. Series: Smithsonian nature book.
QL696.S8N47   598′.97   80-607110
ISBN 0-87474-672-8
ISBN 0-87474-673-6 (pbk.)

Cover   Free again! A newly banded owl in full flight looks for a suitable distant perch.

Frontispiece   When an owl is annoyed or anxious, the bristly feathers surrounding the bill are spread.

Dedicated to John T. Emlen, Jr., professor, mentor, and friend

Contents

Foreword, 8

Preface, 10

Acknowledgments, 12

1. **A Beginning**, 15

2. **Out of the Woods**, 28

3. **An Owl in the City**, 37

4. **To Catch an Owl**, 44

5. **An Elusive Bird**, 57

6. **The Species—A Closer Look**, 69

7. **Short Days and Long Nights**, 85

8. **Feathers on the Snow**, 94

9. **A Time of Change**, 101

10. **A Nesting of Owls**, 113

11. **In Search of Nests**, 123

12. **Nest Builders**, 135

13. **A Different Race of Creatures**, 148

Bibliography, 157

Index, 163

Foreword

The Great Gray Owl stands near the top of every serious bird watcher's most-wanted list. On their periodic forays south into the northern United States, these huge, pale-eyed phantom visitors from the boreal forests bring forth a rush of binocular- and camera-laden voyeurs who study, photograph, and record their every move; subsequently, the owl's quizzical face peers forth from nature magazine covers and stories are told and retold.

In the past such incursions resulted in spates of trophies or specimens displayed in game rooms or deposited in museums. In more recent years, however, a network of telephone information centers has alerted bird watchers to the owls' occurrences south of their usual haunts and has meant that many more persons could enjoy the silent winter visitors. Nevertheless, few scientists have studied their habits on the breeding grounds and little was known of their home lives.

What studies there were, especially in North America, had generally been fortuitous, the result of chance finds of convenient nests. But scientist Bob Nero of the Manitoba Department of Natural Resources and photographer Bob Taylor from Winnipeg doggedly and successfully pursued their quarry in the spruce-tamarack bogs near the United States-Canadian border over a number of years. Their anxious listening for deep hooting and hopeful waiting for the great birds to come winging silently back to the nest for a new season were rewarded. Their work began in earnest—and this book is the result.

Owls have persistently charmed, fascinated, and awed mankind for aeons, and their nighttime calls have struck terror into the superstitious as harbingers of danger or even death. Unlike most birds, owls can look you straight in the eye; their flat faces and large eyes impart an almost human aspect to their physiognomies. The owl was a symbol of wisdom long before Athena's Little Owl first peered defiantly from the tetradrachm, and even today children recite an ode to the "wise old owl." As we learn more about their habits, some of the owls' mystery vanishes, but our fascination persists.

The Great Gray Owl's diet of forest voles hardly seems adequate for such a formidable, long-winged predator, but under its long, dense feather coat lurks only a modest body, hardly bulkier than those of its more temperate cousins, the Barred Owl of North America or the Tawny Owl of Eurasia. Unlike its relatives in the genus *Strix*, it is not entirely nocturnal, but can hunt actively during the day, providing many more hours for it to capture prey in the forest. Also, nesting begins before the trees leaf out, so that, even in the cool early morning hours, there is relatively good light in the forest. These circumstances, and an accessible nest, made it possible for Nero to study the birds' behavior and for Taylor to make his superb photographic record. Furthermore, because of their remote forest habitat, the owls hadn't been exposed to humans and were thus remarkably tolerant of observers. The female incubated the eggs or brooded the young, and the male regularly brought food to the nest, even when Nero and Taylor were visible.

Great Gray Owls must also be competent night hunters, for many stay in the far north all winter, when days are short and few small mammals emerge from beneath the snow. Then the owls' ability to hunt by sound guides them to prey under the surface, where even their keen night vision is of no use. The large facial disc, rimmed with remarkably modified feathers, concentrates sound into the owl's highly directional ears. Cruising silently through the forest, the hunter scans the snow for faint sounds of activity. Broad wing tracings in a soft white blanket of newly fallen snow found by Nero vividly record the tragic end of an unsuspecting vole which thought itself secure in its burrow under the snow.

Over a period of years, Nero and Taylor and their collaborators have pieced together the story of the home life and annual cycle of the owl. It is a fascinating account of adaptation to a special way of life. I first heard of this project in 1975, when the American Ornithologists' Union held its annual meeting in Winnipeg. Nero and Taylor showed the AOU members an early version of their film on the Great Gray Owl; several hundred ornithologists, professional and amateur alike, were held in awe at the trustful nature of their subject. We watched the female take a vole from the male and feed it to the downy white young. And we marveled at the capacity of the chick's maw as it labored to gulp down whole a rodent nearly its own size.

Bob asked me then about the Smithsonian Institution Press and other possible publishers for his study. I encouraged him to submit his manuscript. The result is this book, which now makes the Great Gray Owl one of the better understood large owls and should stir even wider interest among birders for catching a glimpse of one on their next southern foray when winter food becomes scarce in the boreal forests.

George E. Watson, Curator of Birds
National Museum of Natural History
Smithsonian Institution

Preface

Had a different title been used for this book, say, "Gray Owl of the North," some would have assumed that here was yet another biography of "Grey Owl," that semi-mystical Englishman-turned-Indian who carried woodland lore from Canada to England's royal family. That devoted conservationist, despite his Indian-given name, was no particular friend of the owl, which he called "a detestable bird whose name had been imposed on me only on account of my nocturnal habits."

Grey Owl's unkind comments about his namesake probably reflect an older, almost universal view of owls as mournful creatures of darkness, usually of ill omen, an attitude frequently expressed in poetry and prose. Typical is this phrase from "To the Owl" by Robert Burns: "Sad bird of night, what sorrows call thee forth, to vent thy plaints thus in the midnight hour?"

More recently, and in keeping with a changing view of owls, author August Derleth commented: "The lore of owls, I am inclined to think, takes too little notice of such intelligence as the owl surely has; the bird merits a wider appreciation and some course in public instruction designed to teach mankind something more of his way of life."

"Intelligence" may not be the correct word for the behavioral flexibility and learning capacity exhibited by owls, but otherwise I can agree with Derleth's viewpoint. A Long-eared Owl, taken as a fledgling and kept in our home a year for study, taught me that owls are sensitive, playful birds. Changes in its posture and facial appearance gave evidence of a variety of moods, from relaxed docility to aggression and fear. It taunted both our sleepy, old cat and our slightly puzzled spaniel, aggressively hopping across the carpet daringly close to them, one feathered foot in front of the other, while leaning backward in readiness for escape

should either target arouse itself. Muzzle flat to the floor, the dog's main responses to the advancing bird were cocking his eyebrows or flaring his nostrils; the cat's twitching tail suggested a greater emotion, but both seemed to accept the advancing owl as something to be endured, if not appreciated.

Daily I engaged the owl in a hunting game, tossing a tightly rolled ball of yarn onto the floor while the owl watched expectantly from its perch on the curtain rod. Then followed a pause while we watched each other to see which would make the first move, and then a quick dash downward by the owl as I simultaneously reached out for the ball. If I got it first, the owl returned to its perch, shaking out its feathers and readying itself for another try. When it succeeded in snatching up the ball it gave a pleasant cackling call, as close to triumphant laughter as I dared attribute to it, while flying a circular course through the living room and kitchen, back to its perch, the ball clenched in its talons.

The close observations made possible by that captive bird later provided useful insights. When I moved to Winnipeg in 1966 I had no special interest in raptors and had never seen a Great Gray Owl. All I knew about them was that they were rare. I first saw them in 1968 and found them to be captivating birds. Since then I have observed them every year, winter and summer, day and night, in Manitoba and adjacent Minnesota. No other species has so preoccupied my time and attention. This unique species is as much a part of the northern coniferous forest as loon, raven, wolf, or moose.

Almost unseen in some years, at other times they have been relatively common. My colleagues and I have been privileged to see and handle unusually large numbers of Great Gray Owls. We have studied them under more diverse circumstances than can be described. What has impressed me most is their range of expression, their variety of mood and behavior, and their relative docility. It has been not so much a study as a pursuit, but it has been greatly rewarding.

It has not been my intention to describe all the events we experienced or to document all the data we obtained during the period of our study. Technical reports of our joint findings are in preparation for publication in suitable journals. Rather, this book is meant to provide, in addition to a basic account of the natural history of the Great Gray Owl, an opportunity for the reader to share in our experiences.

One has to stop somewhere, and in the main, observations and data in this book do not extend beyond July 30, 1979.

Acknowledgments

For constant companionship in the field and mutual pleasure in studying Great Gray Owls from 1968 to 1980, I am especially indebted to Herbert W. R. Copland, an experienced birder, born and raised in Winnipeg. The good and bad events that Herb Copland and I have shared would make a memorable story. His good humor, patience, and enthusiasm provided invaluable support to our field work. Beverly Copland kindly consented to her husband's participation. Robert R. Taylor, naturalist and free-lance photographer, really got me started on owls. Bob Taylor's photographs, which add so much to this book, reveal his technical skills, and his experience in working with owls. The many hours of assistance given me by my son, Redwood "Woody" Nero, are a rich part of my owl years. His younger brother, Brook, also assisted me.

Raymond Tuokko is a Winnipeg resident, but his folks live near Lac du Bonnet, in an area practically surrounded by Great Gray Owl habitat. From the day I first met Ray on a highway where we were looking for owls, he has actively shared our interest in this bird. Ray's records, observations, and tireless field efforts have been a valuable asset.

Spencer G. Sealy, ornithologist at the University of Manitoba, who arrived in Winnipeg in 1974, soon found himself caught up in our quest. His energy and questioning spirit lent important support to our efforts. K. Michael Collins, working under Spencer toward a Master's degree in zoology, began a two-year study of the Great Gray Owl in 1975. Few of his findings appear here because his thesis is not yet complete. However, I have described a few situations in which we were both involved.

Inspiration and encouragement were provided by Dalton Muir, a Great Gray Owl fan and photographer with whom we spent many hours at an active nest.

Many people provided assistance and information, but special thanks are due the following: Kathleen S. Anderson, Eugene F. Bossenmaier, Soren Bondrup-Nielson, Daniel F. Brunton, Paul M. Catling, Fred Cooke, John Christie, Calvin Cuthbert, Alice Dennis, John Donald, Kim Eckert, David L. Evans, Carl Feilberg and family, Don G. Follen, Sr., Ken Gardner, Robert E. Gehlert, W. Earl Godfrey, Dan Guravitch, David R. M. Hatch, John C. Hellson, Stu Iverson, Paulette J. Henson, Nils Höglund, C. Stuart Houston, Ross D. James, Patricia A. Knipe, Gerry McKeating, Katherine A. McKeever, Heimo Mikkola, William Nakka, Clarence E. Nordstrom and family, Albert F. Oeming, Marianne Page, Al Peden, Richard M. Poulin, Philip B. Reader, James R. Salt, W. Ray Salt, Vere H. Scott, William Sitar, Jack Steinbring, Robert Stitt, Betty Struthers, Jack and Irene Tuokko, Wayne Tuokko, Brian Turner, Jens Wahlstedt, Sam Waller, Ed and Marg Ward, Jon Winter, and Andrew Yakiwchuk.

Grants in support of field work were received from the Seven Sisters Falls Wildlife Association (Manitoba), the Manitoba Naturalists Society, and the Frank M. Chapman Memorial Fund (American Museum of Natural History). Financial support was received as a gift from Al Graham, a former fellow employee with a special fondness for owls. Some support was received initially from the Manitoba Museum of Man and Nature.

From fall 1978 onward, the Manitoba Department of Natural Resources, in which I have been employed as a wildlife specialist since 1970, provided invaluable travel and sustenance support. For this service I am especially grateful to Richard C. Goulden, Director of Wildlife. Information and assistance were received from many of my fellow employees. Regional staff of the Department contributed numerous observations and rendered many useful services. Regional accommodations of the Department were made available to us over the entire period of the study. Immigration and customs officers at Canadian and United States stations at the Manitoba-Minnesota border points of South Junction and Middlebro, Manitoba, rendered many useful services.

Sherryl B. Wilner did much of the typing. Inga Storgaard and Fritz A. Lindberg kindly provided a translation of a Swedish publication.

For critical and helpful comments on an early draft of the manuscript I am indebted to Carol A. Scott. Her enthusiastic response provided incentive when it was badly needed. Special thanks are due Vene Parnell and Mary Ann Rodewald for their insightful and supportive perusal of a late draft. Many hours were spent by Linda L. Safir who skillfully and energetically applied her pen to several drafts. Certain passages owe much to her fine judgment.

I am grateful for comments on the manuscript received from referees for the University of Wisconsin Press and the Smithsonian Institution Press. I am especially indebted to staff of the latter organization for assistance in bringing this book into being, particularly Edward F. Rivinus and Hope Pantell.

In writing the text I have drawn extensively upon the literature, especially in respect to the Great Gray Owl, relying on accounts by ornithologists, birders, and naturalists. Credit is given to authors for cited material, and references are listed in the bibliography. The maps were prepared by Horst Schell.

Finally, I am grateful to my family and particularly to my wife, Ruth, for extended support during the past twelve years. Without her understanding and forbearance it would not have been possible to devote so much of my time to watching owls and writing this book.

1
A Beginning

In a mature stand of trembling aspen beside a massive granite outcrop, long before leaves are out, shadowy figures slip silently back and forth, building a nest high in a weathered old aspen tree. Sleek, bluish-gray Goshawks pile twig upon twig in an upright triad of limbs; many twigs fall to the ground, but day by day the nest grows in size until a compact, interwoven mass eighteen inches across and nearly as deep has been formed. Before the young will have left the nest in midsummer there will be a wide array of colorful feathers beneath it—American Robin, Blue Jay, Common Flicker, and even larger birds falling prey to this species. Fast and powerful, the red-eyed Goshawk is a specialist in capturing forest birds and mammals. With its broad, fan-shaped tail acting as a rudder, it can steer adroitly through thick stands of trees, efficiently pursuing Ruffed Grouse.

Through summer and fall the Goshawk family feeds on woodland birds, reaching out over a wider area with each passing week. In late summer, hordes of migrating birds, intent on foraging in advance of the next night's long flight, are easy prey. In autumn, migration over, the woods are suddenly still. Last year, snowshoe hares and Ruffed Grouse provided an abundant fare, but in this season they are scarce. Driven by hunger, the Goshawks finally move southward into new, distant lands. Two months later, in a woodlot eight hundred miles to the south, the male Goshawk is shot from a perch by a hunter seeking cottontails. A week later, the female Goshawk is shot in a nearby farmyard as it makes a second pass at a flock of wheeling pigeons.

For two years the nest in the aspen grove is unoccupied. In the third year, late in February, a Great Gray Owl, drawn to the aspen woods and adjacent farm fields by an abundance of meadow voles, flies to the snow-covered nest. In the next few weeks it returns again and again, hooting softly in the cold night, and eventually attracting a mate. So the Goshawk nest, deserted for two years, becomes a center of activity for another season, another species.

A hunting male on an aspen branch. This Great Gray Owl is so intent on a mouse beneath the snow that it is barely aware of the photographer. The fine tips of its tail feathers identify the bird as immature; by size it is a male (smaller than the female in nearly all owl species).

In early June 1964 ornithologist David F. Parmelee was told about a nearby Goshawk nest by a friend, Philip B. Reader, whom he was visiting about ten miles north of The Pas in north-central Manitoba. This chance remark led to a visit to the nest—and to the surprising and exciting discovery that instead of Goshawks, it was occupied by Great Gray Owls! It was a first for both men, although Reader, a woodsman and trapper, had lived in that area for most of his life. Parmelee reported: "The mate, after first announcing his arrival by hooting softly, flew from the muskeg directly to the nest with a small rodent. Upon presenting the prey, he quickly flew back to the muskeg on perfectly silent wings and disappeared only to return a short time later. Both birds were decidedly tame—almost indifferent to our presence."

This was only the second Great Gray Owl nest recorded for Manitoba, the first having been found nearly two hundred miles to the south in mid-May by birder Ed Robinson. I learned about the nest at The Pas late in 1964 when Dave Parmelee submitted a nest record card to the provincial museum. Each year thereafter, at my request, Phil Reader checked the nest, but it went unused, and I began to wonder if I would ever see a Great Gray Owl. Then in March 1968 Reader spotted owls near the nest tree, and in April he sent news that the female was on the nest, apparently incubating! In mid-April Robert R. Taylor, then photographer at the Manitoba Museum of Man and Nature, took a crew to the nest site. The group, which included the late Jack D. Herbert, director of the museum, was led to the nest by Reader. Several loads of equipment were carried in through heavy, wet snow, and a tower was erected to support a camera level with the nest. In mid-May 1968, when there were three young in the nest, another trip was made from Winnipeg to The Pas, and I went along, anxious to see my first live Great Gray Owl.

The nest was in the crown of a tall aspen poplar tree in a mature grove of aspen surrounded by black spruce-muskeg. Several leafless, adjacent dead aspens gave the site an open aspect that surprised me. I had expected to see this bird nesting in deep shade, not high up in open sunlight. Upon our arrival, the female left the nest, restlessly moving from one branch to another, gliding lower with each move, finally settling on a snag twenty-five feet high and about fifty yards from the nest tree. At first she faced us, blinking and looking down so steadily she made me uncomfortable. After we arranged ourselves on logs and became quiet, however, she turned her head away, looking toward a bank of spruce trees. With head lowered and back feathers slightly elevated, shifting from one foot to another, she seemed impatient, hooting softly at regular intervals and occasionally emitting a nasal call. Suddenly, as if guided by her voice, the male came flying out of the woods, heading directly toward her. Briefly clinging to the same perch, large wings spread for balance, he gave her a vole, then turned and fled back into the woods. Without a glance our way, the female, vole in bill, flew up into the nest tree, landing on the edge of the nest fifty feet above us. I watched through binoculars with great interest while she fed the vole to one of the nestlings. Though the food exchange sequence passed all too quickly, and would be witnessed again and again, this first view of it was thrilling, and well worth the 500-mile drive from Winnipeg.

Now, with the female at the nest, the young stood up, downy heads visible, calling repeatedly, a nasal, rasping *"Sherrick!"* While we awaited the next visit of the male, Pileated Woodpeckers called from a nearby nest in a large, dead aspen bole; a Common Goldeneye Duck unexpectedly sped through the trees heading for another nest cavity; boreal chorus frogs shrilled almost constantly from pools of meltwater on the forest floor. Sip-

ping hot tea freshly brewed by Phil in a tin pail over a small fire, we congratulated ourselves and gratefully toasted our host. We conversed quietly, seldom taking our eyes off the nest. Finally, with a renewed calling by the female and young, the male arrived again! This time he flapped heavily up to the nest. Scarcely had he landed before the prey he brought was plucked from his bill by the female. Seconds later he dropped away from the nest, sailing off out of our sight through the spruce.

The female, when not brooding or feeding the young, perched at various places in the vicinity of the nest tree, usually on a conspicuous branch or snag. When a light breeze ruffled the long feathers on the back of her head and neck, it looked as if she had a mane; backlighted by the sun, the rippling feathers were luminous. When preening her breast or neck plumage, she would bend forward and seize a feather at its base with her bill, then

slowly draw her bill along the entire length of the feather, raising her head with each smooth stroke. She exhibited a surprising agility when doing this. Though all birds preen, it was pleasing to see the owl doing it. It suggested that she was completely relaxed in our presence.

For the next three days we eagerly studied and photographed these owls, which, for the most part, seemed barely aware of our presence. Once, in later afternoon, the female flew down into shrubbery beneath the trees and we thought she was hunting. But no, she had gone to bathe in a pool. A quick splashing was heard, a moment later she landed on the upright roots of an overturned tree and proceeded to dress her plumage. As she vigorously shook out her wet feathers, her dark, shadowed outline was suddenly surrounded by a spray of sparkling drops of water.

When we stood beneath her and imitated the squeak of a mouse, she would

Opposite: An adult bird in winter. The vertical stripes of the Great Gray Owl's upper body, and horizontal bars of the lower body, are in marked contrast to the reverse pattern in the related Barred Owl.

Above: An owl driven from the forest by hunger sits on a fence post. Falling snow and low light levels bring owls out of the woods into city backyards in search of prey.

turn her head and stare down at us for a moment, bright yellow eyes steady and unwavering; then she would slowly turn and look back toward the nest, and toward the woods where her mate moved on his distant hunting forays. Other birds were of little concern to the owl, though when a soaring Red-tailed Hawk, out of some aggressive fancy, gave a shrill scream and suddenly swooped at the nest, the brooding female, without leaving the nest, gave a loud hoot followed by several rapid and softer notes. Late one evening when the female was away from the nest, a flock of eleven migrant Whistling Swans flew by over the nest tree. The young owls, evidently responding to the sound of the swans' wings, stood up, crying with hunger, mouths wide open as if they expected to be fed.

Wanting photographs of the male bringing food to the female at night, Bob Taylor fastened a remote-controlled camera and flash unit to the top of the tower. He and I sat nearby in the cold night, looking up in the general direction of the nest, relying on vocalizations by the female as a signal to trigger the camera. The male came four or five times, mainly in the early part of the night. When the electronic light flashed, we caught a tantalizing glimpse of the nest—owls, nest, and branches momentarily illuminated. After each photo was taken, Bob patiently climbed the metal rungs of the tower to advance the film for the next shot. Later, looking at the night photos, we found the exercise had been a success. One photo revealed unexpected prey, a wood frog dangling in the male's bill. Best of all, the photos showed owls with fully expanded pupils for night vision. This gave them large, dark eyes, a softer look than we had known.

In early June we returned to the site for a final visit, having been told that the family had disappeared. It was an empty scene. The nest, now just a bundle of twigs, and no longer the focal point of ac-tivity for a pair of owls, was of little interest. We managed, however, to find two of the young, locating them by listening for their rasping hunger calls. Both were several hundred yards from the nest tree and on low perches. But where were the parents? They should have been in sight, hooting and showing annoyance at our presence. Though we stayed near the young owls until past midnight, no adults appeared nor did we see them the next morning. By now both young were weak and, though we force-fed them, they died before the day was over. We finally and reluctantly concluded that both parent birds were dead. The presence of a line of new marking tape right past the nest tree suggested a survey party may have encountered the adults. With young on the ground nearby, the owls would probably have been attentive, perhaps even aggressive. Had they been shot, we wondered, for trophies?

We took the dead owlets along for museum specimens and, thinking it would be a long time before we would see Great Gray Owls again, returned with some disappointment to Winnipeg, far from owl country; or so we thought. That winter, however, to everyone's surprise, large numbers of Great Grays unexpectedly appeared in forested lands not far east of the city. Suddenly we had owls at our doorstep! Before winter was over we were to see more owls than had ever previously been reported in the province. As many as twelve were seen in one day along the Trans-Canada Highway thirty to seventy miles to the east of Winnipeg, and two owls even appeared in the city. Weekends and evenings were spent looking for owls to photograph, trap, count, and just watch, but there was never time enough. We estimated that a hundred owls were present that winter in southeastern Manitoba and northern Minnesota. Though there had been reports of invasions of owls in earlier years, nothing of this magnitude had been observed.

It was overwhelming. Suddenly we had owls in an amusing variety of situations and often close at hand. Great Grays hunted from perches a few feet off the ground, dark bodies prominent against a snow-covered landscape, taking little notice of our presence. Those birds we captured for banding were handled with respect and admiration. In hand, Great Gray Owls are even more imposing; once they ceased struggling, these owls bore our prodding and stroking with haughty disdain. Only after they were released and had flown up to the nearest tree, when they turned and stared back at us, did we sense their annoyance; with a great ruffling of feathers, they rid themselves of our alien touch.

Is it any wonder that my interest in this species has continued to this day? The opportunities to keep looking for owls were too good to resist, and I soon found myself heavily involved in a search for more information about owls in this region. The following winter a much smaller number was observed in essentially the same area; however, a concentration was found just south of the border, in Minnesota, in April 1970, an observation that led to the discovery of an active nest. Thereafter,

from 1968 to 1980, my friends and I concentrated our efforts in extreme southeastern Manitoba and adjacent Minnesota.

The country roughly west of Lake of the Woods and south of Lake Winnipeg became our main study area. Though Winnipeg sits on a vast, intensively cultivated plain, suitable Great Gray breeding habitat lies as close as thirty miles eastward. Here, a band of black spruce and tamarack-muskeg country a few dozen miles wide and a hundred miles from north to south lies adjacent to the rocky Precambrian Shield region. The western margin of this boreal forest lowland is bordered with aspen parkland. Wherever the soil in this area is suitable for agriculture, and sometimes where it is not, the land has been cleared and farmed.

In this area, not far from a metropolitan city of more than half a million, with patience and luck it is possible to find Great Gray Owls. Retiring by nature, fond of deep, secluded woods and bogs, these birds are unseen in many years. Following an increase in population, or when food is scarce, they emerge from the forests in search of prey. A mixture of old burns, cleared forest, marginal cropland, abandoned fields, grassy meadows, pine and

By night and day, an emigrant owl looks over unfamiliar fields and woods.

A tense moment in pursuit of an owl: one man is ready with a net, the other with rod
and lure, as a bird approaches. The trick is to keep the lure (an artificial mouse) moving
just fast enough so that the owl chases it until the bird is close enough to net. Capturing
and banding Great Gray Owls under appropriate scientific permits is an essential way of
gathering information on population size, movements, age and sex ratios, and other
biological data.

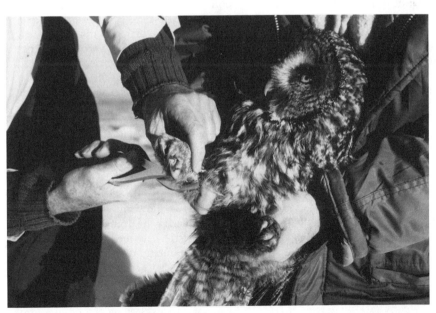

Banding an owl. It is important to hold the bird's feet tightly, ever watchful of the long,
sharp talons, while a numbered aluminum leg band is attached as a permanent means
of identifying individuals.

spruce woods, bogs and streams, the area attracts moose, wolves, Common Ravens, Gray Jays, and many other boreal forest animals.

What is most curious about this southern range is the occurrence of owls in relatively sparse forest cover. Stunted spruce-tamarack stands, not much more than thirty feet in height, for example, would hardly seem to be suitable Great Gray Owl habitat. And yet, birds have nested in this kind of cover, close to roads and logging operations, a far cry from the usual habitat with which the species is so often associated. Is there a relationship between southern tamarack bogs and spruce-tamarack muskegs of the north? Wet tamarack stands east of Winnipeg, for example, are similar in many aspects to the northern transition forest. Robert Stitt, a university student who spent the winters of 1976–77 and 1977–78 trapping in the "great, empty muskegs" west of Moosonee, Ontario, at the southwest corner of James Bay, wrote me that he found the Great Gray Owl the "most frequently seen" of the four species occurring there (Great Horned, Hawk, Boreal, and Great Gray Owls). Although conspicuous in some situations, Great Gray Owls can remain hidden even in the heavily cutover and often burned forests typical of southern Manitoba. Indeed, the transitional aspect of many tracts of forest, altered by fire and cutting, may make these sites especially attractive to owls.

But the area is also divided by several main highways and numerous side roads, many parts are logged continuously, and much of the area is intensively used for recreation in summer and winter. Perhaps nowhere else on the continent are their breeding grounds in such close contact with so much human activity.

Through intensive searching, mainly in winter, spring, and early summer, we discovered that Great Grays were regular residents of this area. Even in years when few were seen, we heard birds calling late at night. This resident population of owls, as we gradually came to understand it, became the focus of our attention.

Made aware of our excitement about owls, many people watched for them with us. Customs and immigration officers, Royal Canadian Mounted Police (RCMP), conservation officers, naturalists, and the general public became acquainted with our studies and interests through posters, newspaper accounts, occasional lectures given in schools and community centers, and through personal contact at every opportunity.

Our search for owls led us into many out-of-the-way places, and in this way we became acquainted with many interesting people. Farmers, loggers, tradesmen, housewives, and children were our informants and friends. Many pleasant hours were spent talking about owls and other subjects with people for whom these woods were familiar grounds. And as we exchanged confidences, so too we exchanged information. Once, reaching the end of a small road that led to a little farmhouse close to spruce-tamarack woods, we chatted with the gruff owner, an unshaven, older man wearing a tattered parka and black rubber boots. After telling him why we were looking for big owls, we asked if he had seen any. In broken English he told us that for several days during the bitter cold weather of the previous week, one had come each day to sit on the power pole beside his house. Yes, he said, it looked just like the owl in the photo we showed him. He thought it was hungry, because it had been a hard winter, with lots of snow and few mice. With evident sincerity, he argued that the government should help feed wildlife in winter, including hungry owls.

Another day, we drove several miles along a narrow logging trail. Neat stacks of freshly cut spruce logs stood about the edge of a large clearing devoid of all but a few spindly tamaracks and low heaps of spruce boughs. Seeing a man in rough clothing working beside a machine, we parked and walked over to talk with him; the cold air was redolent with the sharp, pleasant scent of spruce and cedar. When we asked about the presence of owls, we were given a hard look and firmly told that no owls would be shot by us or anyone else in his presence! We hastened to explain our interest in owls and then shook hands all around in support of his point of view.

One cold morning on the Trans-Canada Highway, Bob Taylor and I saw a police car with a flashing red light coming up behind us, and we anxiously asked each other what we could possibly have done. We pulled off the road and stopped, and were stunned (and relieved) when the RCMP officer shouted that we should follow him back the other way because he had just seen a Great Gray Owl! Following his lead, we did a fast turnaround and sped down the highway behind our excited escort. I don't recall if we caught that owl or not, but I well remember the incident. That kind of cooperation from someone we had spoken to twenty minutes earlier in a coffee shop is a good example of the response we got from people when we told them about our project.

Frequently, upon making enquiries, we were invited in to warm ourselves or to share a meal. The enthusiasm with which the members of a family would tell us about owls they had seen made these enjoyable events. Oh, there were other kinds of people as well! I won't forget the pretty, well-spoken woman who told me she had indeed seen a really big owl sitting in a tree near the barn, "one of those big gray fellows; it sat right out in the open, tame as could be . . . how I wished I had a gun . . . it would really have looked nice stuffed!"

Below: An owl with a painted tail hovers over a shadow-striped snowbank. Spray painting the tail feathers of banded birds makes it possible to identify banded and unbanded owls in a winter population. Painting is a temporary marking method, lasting until the tail feathers are shed in summer.

Opposite: Hunting the hunter—two men with owl-catching gear in hand try to get closer to an actively hunting bird in the woods. Trapping and handling seem not to have much lasting effect on Great Gray Owls; banded and tail-painted birds may be hunting again within minutes after their release.

2

Out of the Woods

Characterized by trees, shrubs, and numerous other plants that are green in winter as well as summer, the boreal forest is adapted to a short growing season. Evergreen—what a wealth of impressions that name brings forth. Compared with the brown, muddy fields and drab vegetation that appear with spring in southern parts, the evergreen world of the boreal forest is a revelation. Beneath the snow the forest floor is carpeted in green. Feather mosses, club moss, Labrador tea, bunchberry, and a host of other green plants lie beneath the embracing arms of pine, spruce, fir, and cedar; all are chlorophyll machines perpetually in gear, ready to take advantage of daylight once winter loosens its hold. On the coldest day in midwinter, though their trunks are iron-fast and their veins immobilized with cold, the evergreen forests stand heavy and lush with foliage.

There is comfort in the heavy mass of spruce that surrounds us as we ski through the woods, comfort in the absence of wind, and in the close contact with winter birds that approach us with curiosity. A flock of Boreal Chickadees, briefly pausing in their prying inspection of limbs and twigs, repeatedly call: "Dee-dee!"—fluttering about us when we softly squeak to draw them close. Gray Jays, light as down and fluffed out like thistle heads, come to visit us, dropping down in slow, almost motionless glides, then loosely hopping from one perch to another, whistling and chattering.

Though it is thirty degrees below zero, a sudden, sharp sense of springtime bird song halts us: a Pine Grosbeak in cheerful red plumage, perched on a wiry black spruce spire, delivers his sweet, flutelike call. How, we wonder, do these winter birds find enough food to sustain themselves? Moving lightly and quickly, they seem without cares; but they are constantly on the move, seaching for food as they go through the forest, and this is part of their adaptation to long, cold winters.

Few other birds that nest within the boreal forest of North America have been sought so energetically by birdwatchers as has the Great Gray Owl. According to the American Birding Association (which numbers more than 3,000 members in North America), the Great Gray Owl is the sixth most wanted bird on the continent. Occasionally, these birds wander in winter outside their usual range to southern parts of Canada and the northern United States. When the news gets out, enthusiastic birders may travel hundreds of miles in hopes of seeing one of these owls.

In the winters of 1965–66 and 1968–69, for example, a few Great Gray Owls in the Ottawa area attracted hundreds of birders from all over the eastern United States and across southern Ontario and Quebec. In the winter of 1977–78, when large numbers of owls appeared in the Duluth, Minnesota, area, hundreds of birders from many midwestern states drove there to see Great Gray, Boreal, and Hawk owls. Great Gray Owls made headlines in the winter of 1978–79 when several birds appeared in New York State. During the same period, unusual numbers were seen in the New England states and especially in southern Ontario and Quebec. Close to forty Great Gray Owls were recorded on Amherst Island in the St. Lawrence River near Kingston, Ontario. A thousand birders from as far away as New Jersey, Maryland, and Texas came to Amherst Island that winter. Several happy birders were able to see both the eclipse of the sun and Great Gray Owls, which were present in considerable numbers east of Winnipeg in late February 1979.

A single Great Gray Owl that appeared on January 22, 1973, at Gill, Massachusetts, and lingered on at the same farm until mid-March, attracted the attention of an estimated two hundred eager searchers each weekend and ten each weekday. Conservatively, perhaps three thousand people looked for this one bird, and two thousand saw and enjoyed it! How is one to measure the value of such a bird? In 1978 the United States government published a set of postage stamps bearing illustrations of four species of owls: Sawwhet, Great Horned, Barred, and Great Gray. That the Great Gray Owl should have been chosen despite the several more common species of owls in the United States is an indication of its appeal.

The thrill that invariably accompanies a Great Gray Owl sighting is shared by neophyte and experienced ornithologist; it is related to this bird's general scarcity, its great size, and its boldness. Few birds look upon people with the apparent calm stoicism of Great Gray Owls. Perched for hours on a roadside tree or telephone pole, they are unmoved by hundreds of passing vehicles; a noisy snowmobile passing directly underneath an owl may not even draw a glance; at times, dozens of photohungry naturalists may approach within yards without flushing the bird. Filled with my own impressions formed during many hours in the company of Great Gray Owls, I can appreciate the reactions of other people who have encountered this species.

Commenting in the *Winnipeg Tribune* on a bird that appeared in the city in November 1959, nature columnist Angus H. Shortt noted that it "showed a great deal more concern about a passing train and aeroplanes flying overhead, than about the bird watchers standing only a few yards away." And, after observing wintering birds in the Alymer, Quebec, area in 1966 amd 1969, Ronald Pittaway and Daniel F. Brunton wrote: "The Great Gray Owl is absurdly tame. If the bird doesn't feel like flying, it *cannot* be moved (short of being shot!). Repeatedly, one of them has flown directly past observers, within inches of them without changing its direction or course whatsoever. It is often the case that the bird is difficult to interest in even looking in the direction of the observer."

Observing a winter vagrant near Ded-

Below: Almost close enough to net! Blood on the bill of this owl, gliding in after a lure that has just been cast to capture it, shows that it had taken real prey minutes before this picture was made.

Opposite: An owl flies down off its perch on a telephone pole toward the live mouse beside the net. A responsive bird may be caught in less than a minute.

ham, Massachusetts on February 7, 1904, Francis H. Allen reported in an ornithological journal: "I was attracted to the spot by a great clamor of Crows and soon found my bird perched on a low limb of a white pine in open mixed woods. It held in its claws a dead and partly eaten crow.... The owl seemed perfectly fearless of me, but showed nervousness when the crows cawed near by, and followed with its eyes the flight of the single crows that flew over its tree from time to time. I drove it about from tree to tree with snowballs. It flew low and always took a rather low perch—from ten to twenty feet from the ground, and usually on a large branch of a pine tree, near the trunk, though twice it alighted on the very top of a red cedar. I could get as near as the height of its perch permitted and was frequently within twenty feet of it during the hour or two that I spent in its company."

Naturalist-farmer Archibald D. Henderson, writing in 1923 about his experiences with these owls on their northern Alberta breeding grounds, remarked: "The Great Gray Owl is not at all a wary bird and always permits a close approach. All that saves him from extermination in the settled districts is the fact that he is seldom seen away from the heavy timber which is his home." That it still retains its peculiar, inherent fearlessness in the presence of man is shown by a recent successful nesting only thirty miles southeast of Edmonton, Alberta. Visiting the nest, which was "within a mile of one of the most heavily used public beaches in central Alberta" on May 5, 1972, Norbert G. Kondla, who discovered the nest, wrote: "Both adult birds were constantly present and seemed quite unafraid of the mob of observers.... Despite the large number of observers on May 5 and many subsequent visits by other observers, the owls managed to raise two young...."

John Christie, a Winnipeg birder, found an even more unlikely nesting in 1979.

Great Gray Owls had successfully occupied a conspicuous nest twenty-five yards from the edge of a road. There was little traffic, but the nest site was only two miles from a main highway. My first reaction on seeing the nest was one of disbelief. It had been built on top of a large "witches'-broom," an abnormal growth of twigs in a tight mass resulting from infestation by the parasitic plant mistletoe. The nest, probably built by a Red-tailed Hawk, was about twenty-five feet above ground in a nearly dead balsam fir, surrounded by low willow, alder, spruce, and tamarack, and knee-deep water. Only a few people knew about the nest, and it was kept secret in hopes of seeing it succeed despite the precarious situation. Fortunately, it did succeed. On June 30 we banded two fledged young and the female, and watched them move off safely into adjacent aspen woods.

Few people have been privileged to see the Great Gray Owl at its nest. The periodic emigrations of Great Grays are periods of hope for birdwatchers, the best chance of seeing one being when these owls come out of the boreal forest, hungry and lean, though still massive in their grayish-brown coats. F. Napier Smith, in a letter in the *Montreal Daily Star*, eloquently described such a meeting in late afternoon, February 12, 1928, near an island in the St. Lawrence River not far from Montreal:

"The wind came in gusts out of the north, driving little clouds of snow along the surface of the river, but despite the icy blasts and the bleak position of its outlook, the Great Grey, apparently a female, sat at perfect ease in her luxuriant coat of feathers ... when I first viewed her, she blended softly with the neutral grey background of the bare hardwood trees on the island. But as I came alongside the island, she stood out boldly against the opalescent wintry sky, the abnormally large, round head giving the bird a top-heavy appearance.... At a distance, the bird ap-

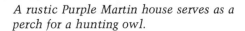
A rustic Purple Martin house serves as a perch for a hunting owl.

peared to be of a solid grey color but at fifty yards or so, in the sunlight, the mottling of the feathers was discernible, although I was unable to detect the small lemon yellow eyes without field glasses. . . . If she appeared huge in the stunted tree growth she looked a veritable 'eagle-owl' as she flew toward the Verdun shore, alighting some 150 yards away on a rise in the ice . . . the large wings and tail and dark coloration emphasizing her size as she skimmed over the surface of the snow.''

In cold winter months when they occasionally visit settlements, Great Grays take to TV antennas, houses, barns, telephone poles, fenceposts, and various other man-made perches as freely as if long accustomed to these things. Few raptors have rested with such impunity on so many peculiar perches or so close to man, but Great Gray Owls move into settled areas as unconcernedly as swallows. David Lambeth, a North Dakota birder visiting southern Manitoba in late winter 1979, wrote that he could hardly believe that Great Gray Owls could be ''as common and conspicuous as Red-tailed Hawks.''

Some things defy explanation. For ten years we never saw an owl perch on a powerline or telephone wire. Then, on December 2, 1978, we saw one fly through trees to land on the lowest of several telephone wires. There were a few seconds when we weren't sure it would maintain its balance, for the wire was swinging and the bird was teetering back and forth, tail spread wide and swinging forward, but it managed to balance itself and sat quietly as we drove by. Thereafter, to my continued amazement, throughout the winter on numerous occasions, we saw birds perched on wires. Moreover, we received reports from several observers who saw them in similar situations and even a hundred miles from our main study area. When a bird landed on a wire close to a pole, or on a heavy cable, it had little difficulty balancing, but those birds that chose to land on a single-strand wire midway between poles went through some vigorous contortions to bring themselves to a standstill. Overnight, it seemed, Great Gray Owls had acquired a new habit.

At The Pas Ed Johanson, a resident with a landscaped yard, described to me how one winter a Great Gray Owl came for weeks and sat for long periods on top of a pole near a bird feeder just outside the picture window. It paid little attention to birds at the feeder, and presumably was after mice attracted by sunflower seeds. At other times it perched on garden stakes and preyed on mice at a backyard compost heap. These large owls have also appeared in yards far from their breeding habitat. For people used to seeing robins or meadowlarks, the sight of a huge owl in the daytime is a spectacular event. Not far from Winnipeg, a housewife photographed a Great Gray Owl through a window. The color photo she sent me shows the owl perched in a tree close to the house.

Great Gray Owls seem to be attracted to people, just as is the Gray Jay, an opportunist always on the alert for food. Still, something else brings jays close to us. I tossed part of a sandwich onto the snow one day for a jay perched near my car, then sacrificed a cookie, but to my

An over-the-shoulder glance, just to see what's happening.

surprise the jay ignored the food. When I left the car to go off through the woods, however, the jay followed me, flying along and perching just overhead. Curiosity—or what? Great Gray Owls sometimes sit and watch woodcutters at work in the forest as if they enjoyed man's company—or are they perhaps awaiting mice driven out by fallen trees?

One acquaintance told me that on November 20, 1978, while out moose hunting near Lac du Bonnet, Manitoba, wearing the prescribed uniform of white coveralls and a blaze-orange cap, he was followed for half an hour by a Great Gray Owl. The bird kept close to him as he moved from one stand to another, sometimes perching on stumps as close as ten feet. Robert Stitt found Great Gray Owls "very tame and curious" near Moosonee, Ontario. On December 22, 1978, he wrote to me as follows:

"Upon returning to camp at dusk I saw the outline of a Great Gray Owl ahead of me near our camp, which is in a narrow band of spruce along the river bank levees in this part of the country. At this point I was in open muskeg. I hurried into camp on the possibility that there was sufficient light for photos. On reaching camp I discovered 3 of the birds very close to our tent. One of the birds seemed very curious and at one point was walking down a limb over my head and making low hooting calls. There was insufficient light for photos so I went back out to the open muskeg to check a marten cubby which I had passed upon first seeing the owl. The distance back out to this cubby was approximately 100 yards. One of the owls flew this distance and perched at the top of a dead spruce at the base of which was my cubby. As I was kneeling down repairing the cubby I could look straight up and see the bird directly above me, peering down on me. This was quite an interesting experience for me. When I returned to camp, and was moving about getting wood, water, etc., the owls were moving from tree to tree and showed interest in what I was doing."

Heavy-headed and long-tailed, a Great Gray has a shape unlike that of any other bird. Perched in the open or outlined against the skyline, its characteristic form can be identified almost as far away as it can be seen. Close up, the round, silvery-gray face and conspicuous white neck stripes are distinctive. Owing partly to the heavy feathering of the head and neck, the bright yellow eyes seem small and close set. Even though it looks like the big bird it is when perched, the size of its wings when it takes flight is still surprising. Spanning nearly five feet, the broad wings expand with ease, flapping deeply as they send the owl off with a rush, giving it, as more than one observer has noted, a heronlike appearance in flight. Upon landing on a new perch, the wings are carefully folded into place, and again one sees the familiar, blunt-headed silhouette of the Great Gray Owl.

For several years we had all accepted the fact that Great Grays occasionally landed and perched in awkward situations, sometimes with tail askew or one wing out, as a consequence of a branch interfering with normal posture. This sometimes is the case, but watching a female owl perched in a willow bush one April morning in 1979, I suddenly realized that the bird was deliberately keeping one wing spread in order to maintain its balance on the slender branches. When the owl changed position, it closed its wing, but when it began to slip, it put one wing out on top of the willow twigs, thus keeping itself upright. That revelation also brought to mind Jens Wahlstedt's report of a Great Gray Owl that nested successfully in 1973 on top of a tall birch stump: the bird constantly supported itself on this unusually small nest platform by resting one wing on a protruding strip of bark.

Despite its bulky appearance, broad wings, and long tail, the Great Gray is a masterful flier, remarkably fast and adept. At times it suddenly brakes in midflight, wings flopping loosely as it wheels about, quickly changing course to pounce upon a mouse unexpectedly popping out of the grass. With wings only partly spread, it can move its wing tips in a rapid, shallow manner like a falcon, quickly attaining high speed. We noted that a bird gliding with wings fully extended, occasionally would partly fold its wings, thus immediately increasing its speed. I have seen owls fly through dense stands of trees, through passageways seemingly too small to admit a bird of this size, abruptly closing their wings to slip through a narrow space, then spreading them out again when clear. They can also time their wingbeats to avoid striking trees.

The most noticeable aspect of their flight behavior, however, is the slow, almost effortless glide with which they move from one perch to another. With a dive off a perch and a few powerful flaps of its wings, a Great Gray is capable of gliding onward for hundreds of yards, silently skimming on broad, outstretched wings across meadows and openings in the forest. An occasional flap or two serves to maintain forward momentum, change direction, or help it rise up to a perch, but otherwise it moves as a shadow. As described so well by Dalton Muir: "Its wings are thick and deep for slow speed flight. It prefers to glide great distances on set wings, close to the ground through the galleries between trees, seldom flapping and steering with obvious tilting with its long, broad tail . . . a vivid demonstration of the efficiency that can be achieved by a perfectly formed aerodynamic shape moving at a speed just sufficient to keep airborne . . . [it] has perfected low speed, silent, manoeuverable flight as a way of life."

Albert F. Oeming of Edmonton, who had carried out an extensive publicity campaign to protect Great Gray Owls in Alberta in the 1950s, also noted the unusual flight manner of these birds: "They were slow, measured and soft, giving the bird an eerie wraith-like appearance as he glided through the great shadowy trees. Although dusk was imminent, if he had been 'as blind as an owl,' as the story goes, the lingering light would have had him crashing into twigs and branches—for his wings were huge billowing sails. They were of such a size as to seem clumsy for life in a dense forest, but he missed branches by a fraction of an inch, making skillful use of this equipment evolved through the ages."

Kapten Wahlberg, observing a female at a nest forty miles north of the Arctic Circle in Sweden, commented on this same aspect: "When she flew with slow lissom strokes between the trees, I thought it very curious that she did not collide somewhere. This is a bird as big as a male Golden Eagle . . . and it was quite amazing to see her flying low in that rather thick wood."

Occasionally their wings do strike branches or twigs, but because the pinions are so soft and flexible, no serious harm seems to result. My observations of birds with one or more broken flight feathers, however, suggest that accidental collisions sometimes cause damage.

One winter day when we were attempting to capture a barely visible owl that was screened by tree branches next to a road, I was startled to see the owl respond to a lure by flying directly through the branches instead of flying around the tree. In its haste to get at the lure, it crashed straight through the branches, snapping off twigs as it came. We caught the bird, and were surprised to find it undamaged. There is another situation in which owls seem reckless about the state of their feathers. Nesting females, when badly upset by the presence of a dog, often go into an astonishing display, hurling themselves onto shrubbery and thrashing their wings against boughs with such force that one would think their flight feathers would break.

In low light at dawn or twilight, the course of a Great Gray Owl's flight is difficult to follow as it glides through shadows and groves and against dark spruce clumps. Even while watched, it may suddenly disappear, but if one follows its line of flight, the eye may catch its flapping wings at some distant point as it reaches for balance on a precarious perch. Once it has gained its balance and is still, it is again easily lost to view, for the woods are full of owl-like shapes.

3
An Owl in the City

Day and night the owl crouched and listened, but the forest was still. Occasionally its attention was drawn to a faint rustle and sigh, as if some hidden vole had suddenly let out its breath. Then the great round head turned down toward the ground, its ears measuring every remote shifting sound beneath the snow. It had not eaten in two weeks.

So it began to move, drifting farther and farther from its natal grounds, searching constantly for the sounds of prey: the pitch-pipe squeal of aggression, the squeak of excitement, the steady, grating gnawing of tiny teeth. But everywhere it went, across snow-covered fields, through open woods, down a tree-lined rivercourse, it found only cold silence.

Often, in the daytime, Black-capped Chickadees and other winter birds chirped and whistled notes that brought the owl to attention, eyes gleaming, but it stayed perched while they flitted past, twittering faintly as they disappeared into woods or field. Once, long before daybreak, a brown shrew skittered across a snowdrift like a leaf in the wind, and at once the owl swooped, snapped it up without landing, and sailed up to a perch. Its bill opened, and in one gulp the shrew was gone.

Driven by hunger, the owl moved onward, drifting over fencelines, skimming beneath power lines, flapping over a cold, bleak cemetery to land in a lone tree. But in the whole area nothing moved. Streets, houses, blocks of human habitations expanded in its vision, and were absorbed as novel but meaningless patterns. Before the sun rose, a strange hum became an insistent drone, strange, confusing sights and sounds of cars and trucks moving in all directions, surrounded by vaporous clouds, gradually overwhelming its senses.

Starving, reduced to a remnant of its normal weight by many days of frantic search, its eyes lost their shine, its movements lessened. Perched on a tree in the middle of the city, shocked by a great rumbling, hissing, and metallic shrieking, the owl subsided, sinking deeper into itself. Sleep, the sleep of hunger, drew it slowly into a stupor. It blinked occasionally when sudden sharp sounds struck its ears, but soon it was motionless, eyes closed, feathers fluffed out, hunched on a limb, lost in an unknown world.

While at the office during a midafternoon snowfall on January 10, 1975, I received news of a supposed Great Gray Owl seen in an older, established residential district in Winnipeg. It seemed unlikely because there had been few reports of Great Grays anywhere that season. However, the caller, John Badertscher, said he had positively identified it. Though it had since disappeared, somewhere among houses and streets, it was just the excuse I needed to leave the office early on a Friday afternoon.

While I dashed home to get a net and some live mice, Herb Copland and several other birders went to try to find the owl. Forty minutes later we were all standing in the snow looking at a bona fide Great Gray Owl dozing on the trunk of a misshapen elm, only ten feet off the ground, beside a garage in a back lane. We hastened to try to capture the bird before it disappeared again, using a live mouse and a landing net, but we couldn't rouse it. After letting the mouse loose on the snow, I made squeaking sounds, scratched on the side of the garage, and muttered a variety of comments to the owl, but it wouldn't open its eyes. It was frustrating. Then it occurred to us to use a ladder, and net the owl where it sat, apparently asleep. A ladder was found beside someone's garage and we were soon in position. But suddenly, when another person came running up to see the action, the owl spread its wings and flew away, heading straight down the lane, looking bigger than ever against a background of two- and three-story houses, garages, power poles, and a multitude of wires. We watched with dismay as it narrowly skimmed a wire, then glided low down the length of the lane, swerving upward at a cross street over the top of several moving cars. In a moment it was out of sight, and we weren't sure which way it had turned. Seven birders again scattered to search for the owl. Traffic, which at this hour was heavy on all streets, plus the heavy snowfall, made it difficult to get about, and we weren't certain we would see the bird again.

Half an hour later, however, after disconsolately combing five city blocks, and rapidly getting cold and tired, I discovered the owl hunched on a post, eyes tightly closed, on a low porch about fifteen feet from a young man who was vigorously sweeping snow off his car. So short of breath I could barely speak, I pointed out the owl—which he hadn't noticed—and urged the astonished man to keep an eye on it while I ran back to my car for the mice and net. "What'll I do if it flies away?" he asked. "Just tell me which way it went!" I shouted back while hurrying off through the falling snow. A few minutes later I was back at the scene and, while my new acquaintance watched with broom in hand, I quickly walked through the soft snow up behind the owl and dropped the net over it. After a brief struggle I had its feet firmly held, then freed it from the net, folded its wings and cradled it against my chest, meanwhile giving a running explanation of our interest in the bird and its habits. Then, clutching net and mouse cage, and carrying the owl upright in the crook of one arm with the top of its head against my chin, I happily set off to my car. A trio of schoolboys passed me on the sidewalk along a busy street, doing a double take and then stopping to argue over whether the bird was alive or not, one of them insisting he had seen it blink its eyes. I left them wondering, and hurried on. Several minutes later a delighted group of birders gathered about to photograph the bird and watch the banding operation.

That evening the owl was subjected to a lot of disturbance. After it was photographed twice by local newspapers, we measured, weighed, and color-marked it. It seemed only slightly alarmed by the flash of the electronic lights, people talking, and the warm, dry new surroundings, maintaining a steadfast staring expression, and making little effort to move so long as its feet were held firmly and it was kept in an upright position. Though we hadn't intended to confine it for long, a week passed before we were able to release it. Our plans had been to hold it overnight and free it in the morning in suitable habitat east of Winnipeg, for we doubted that it would survive long in the city. Unfortunately, the first blizzard of the season struck the region that night, keeping us snowbound for forty-eight hours, unable to get out in the country until the following weekend.

Later, we learned that the owl had been sighted at noon, on the day of its capture, by twelve-year-old Becky Walker while she was going home from school for lunch. Walking down a lane she and two friends were startled when, coming from behind, a small cat ran close beside them on one side while a large, gray owl swooped by on the other side, only a few feet away. The owl landed on a post and the cat escaped. Later, eleven-year-old Betsy Badertscher found the owl perched in a nearby tree and told her parents about it, and thus it was reported to us.

The first time Great Gray Owls were reported in Winnipeg was the winter of 1922–23. The late Harold Mossop, a well-known Winnipeg naturalist, told me that that winter, when he was a teen-aged boy and a keen birder, he had seen possibly twenty owls while on his way to school and while hiking about in wooded sections of the city on weekends. In 1966, in an account of the event in the *Winnipeg Free Press*, he recalled: "an invasion occurred in the Winnipeg area when, because of their lack of fear of man, numbers were shot by irresponsible gunners." One Great Gray Owl from that period exists as a scientific study skin in the collection of the Riveredge Foundation in Calgary, Alberta. The specimen was col-

lected on October 30, 1922 (about four weeks before I was born), in the Charleswood section of Winnipeg where I now make my home!

Not until 1959 was another Great Gray reported in the city. Found near Omand's Creek on November 21, the "big bird stayed in the vicinity throughout the day and was seen and photographed by several local ornithologists," according to an item in the *Winnipeg Tribune* by Angus Shortt. What was possibly the same bird was found a month later suffering from gunshot wounds in Charleswood (!); not long afterward it died in captivity. The bird had been discovered by fourteen-year-old Jorma Jyrkkanen, whose family had re-

cently arrived in Canada from Finland where his father had seen Great Gray Owls. His parents recently informed me that at the time Jorma had found the owl he was already caught up in nature study. Now he is a biologist!

Though our owl evidently had been in the city for at least two weeks, having been seen by other persons, it was in reasonably good condition. It weighed slightly under two pounds, a fair weight for what we judged to be a male bird, but it came to us with an empty stomach—at least it cast no pellet until the day after it had eaten a white laboratory mouse. The little regurgitated lump of yellowish hair and bones found beneath its perch the next morning showed how fast digestion takes place in raptors.

It sat quietly on its perch for hours while we watched television, all of us occasionally glancing over at this novelty in the house. Keeping the owl in captivity gave me a good opportunity to watch it closely. That first weekend, especially, when traffic was at a standstill and we were kept indoors by a blizzard, I sat in comfort with notebook in hand, studying my uncommon subject. It was an entertaining and instructive situation. I learned that the width of its head and neck changed as it raised and lowered its feathers. Depending on its mood it alternated between rapt attention and withdrawn indifference. At times, it tipped back its head and was motionless; it seemed then to be listening to distant sounds, responding to some mechanical sound in the house—the hum of a refrigerator motor or a dripping faucet—as if reminded of some more normal sound of significance. When it shook out its plumage, hunching forward, raising its wings slightly and ruffling its feathers, it gave an impression of composure; thus, its comfort-shake never failed to make me feel better for seeing the owl relaxing. It called infrequently, mostly when we first entered the room in which it was kept, giving a low, mellow *"hoo-hoooh!"* Sometimes it gave this in response to imitations of its call or when the dog or cat suddenly appeared. Whether this was in greeting or in defiance we could not tell. Some of the pleasure in the close relationship I enjoyed with this owl may be seen in the following notes made at the time:

"I could spend hours looking at this bird, seeking to further understand its compelling appearance and behavior. It is a beautiful bird. It sits on a cedar stump in the middle of the family room, tethered by a leather thong. It is twenty-four hours since it was so rudely captured and it has just taken its first meal: two chunks of fresh beef and a dead white mouse. It takes these items directly from my hand, glaring at me all the while with pale yellow eyes, but with little hesitation. Now it seems more relaxed. Last night, when I showed the owl to the surprised family, our trembling dog and the electrified cat, it was docile and unalarmed, permitting itself to be stroked endlessly, almost as if in a trance. Only when I repeatedly pushed my head toward its face did it show any alarm or aggression; then it hissed, and clacked its bill, snapping the lower mandible against the curved upper bill. Finally, it turned its head sideways and nibbled and pulled at my hair, literally preening. Each time I pushed the top of my head toward its face it stretched out its neck, tilted its head and nibbled rapidly along the scalp through my hair, occasionally holding and pulling gently in the hair—a curious behavior. Only when it suddenly seized the edge of my ear, pinching hard, did it hurt me at all. All this while, it also held its wings out from the body, normally a sign of aggressiveness.

"Sitting four feet from the owl, able to watch it closely, I am less able to fathom the bird or my feelings toward it. It watches me as steadily as I watch it, unmoving, except for its eyes: occasionally the nictitating membrane, a semitransparent 'third eyelid' found in all birds, flicks downward from the upper and inner corner of each eye. This gives a startling effect, like a wink without closing the eye, but mostly its eyes are steady and arresting. It is difficult to avoid staring back at the owl. For an hour now we have watched each other, though at times the owl looks off to one side slightly, or briefly closes its eyes by bringing the lower lid up, or else it squints, closing both eyes until the merest slit of yellow shows. Surprisingly, when, without making any other movement, I open my eyes wide, the owl at once opens its eyes too. But it seems to want to sleep; gradually its attention wanes, its lower eyelids slowly come up, the pupils contract, and the eyes are finally almost closed. But when I turn a page, or merely turn my head, it opens its eyes wide again. It is much aware of me even when it appears not to be."

The indifferent and calm state of the Great Gray Owl in captivity is nicely illustrated by an experience related by Alex G. Lawrence in a nature column in the *Winnipeg Free Press*, on March 15, 1928. This, his first view of a Great Gray, occurred in Winnipeg in 1911 "when one of these huge owls was placed on a perch in a drug store window, together with a notice asking if the bird were alive or stuffed. There was a large crowd in front of the window, some members of which stated they had seen the bird move, although it had every appearance of being a stuffed specimen. The owl remained absolutely motionless; not a tremor was noticeable, not a blink of an eye, not a single sign of the bird's breathing; it displayed not the slightest interest in the crowd pressing against the window, and finally, it paid no attention to any scratching on the woodwork, a trick to which a caged owl will nearly always react.

"After ten minutes' steadfast gazing at the bird we were convinced that it was a stuffed specimen, when suddenly the bird sprang to life, stretched its wings, turned its head and yawned amidst the laughter of the crowd. Doubtless many readers will remember being 'stung' by this bird's statue-like posing."

That incident is reminiscent of James Thomas Field's poem "The Owl-Critic," in which a young man in a barber shop delivers a long harangue about the poor workmanship of an owl perched on a shelf. " 'Do take that bird down; have him stuffed again, Mr. Brown!' " he exhorts. Then follow several verses in which the faulty arrangement of all parts of the owl, including its glass eyes, are pointed out by the self-declared owl specialist. The poem ends with the owl arousing itself and suddenly getting down off its perch.

Presumably Lawrence's drugstore bird had been captured in midwinter, possibly even within the city, though he did not say, and was no doubt as hungry and desperate, reduced to conserving its strength, as the bird I kept in our home. On its second day in captivity, our bird again readily accepted chunks of raw beef that were held out before its bill, seeming to recognize these items as food, or responding to the gesture of something held out before it as had been the case throughout its nestling and juvenile life. When a House Sparrow that died overnight in our bird feeder was offered to the owl, it was seized and held by one foot; when I came closer, the owl threatened me, spreading its wings, snapping its bill and glaring intently. Defending the sparrow, still clenched tightly in the talons of one foot, it crouched low on the carpet, covering its prey.

Over the next few days, as it consumed more food, and multi-vitamin capsules concealed in meat, the owl become increasingly aggressive and restless, pulling at its leash and flapping about on the floor around its perch. Left alone, it seemed to spend all of its time trying to free itself. I never knew where it would be when I entered the room after an absence. Once free of the leash it might be perched on the couch, on the back of a chair, or on the bookcase; or, if not free, it was often tangled in its leash. As I neared it to untangle it or to capture and refasten it to the leash, it would rear back with a fierce look, snapping and hissing and flapping its wings. It seemed more and more uncomfortable and unfriendly; clearly the time had come to release it.

Just a week after we had brought it indoors, Herb Copland, Bob Taylor, and I drove fifty miles east of Winnipeg and down a winter logging trail until we reached a black spruce-muskeg site where Great Grays had previously been seen. It looked like a suitable place to release our bird, and we hoped that it would soon find companionship among its own kind.

Though everything was covered with soft, flaky, newly fallen snow, on the sides of drifts in an open, grassy area we found mouse trails and burrows of mice, a heartening sign that the owl would find prey in the vicinity.

Carefully untying the owl's tether for the last time, I held the bird while its portrait was taken against the wintry backdrop of dark spruce. Finally, and with some reluctance, I gave it a gentle toss and it was on the wing. Its broad wings beating heavily at first as it sought to gain momentum, the owl moved rapidly across the snow-covered clearing, heading straight toward a dead tamarack, a lone, leaning pole that seemed to have immediately caught its attention. The owl swooped up onto the pole, landing with graceful precision right on the tip, flapped its wings twice to steady itself as the pole swayed, then folded its wings and was still. . . . Suddenly it was all owl again, wild, beautiful, free. It gave a heavy comfort-shake, ruffling and settling its plumage, and we knew it was back in its own world. It turned its head about and stared briefly toward us, then left its perch and steadily flew off toward the nearby bank of spruce trees, lifted easily over their ragged tops, and was lost to sight.

4
To Catch an Owl

—Excerpt from a letter to the author from Mrs. Elsie Carlson, Pine Falls, Manitoba, February 20, 1974.

"I was looking from my kitchen window in our mobile home which is nestled in a bluff of trembling aspen (poplar) and birch. . . . I noticed a black object near a fence. The background was all deep snow and the black object aroused my curiosity. My husband and I then both observed the black object with a pair of binoculars. The object suddenly took the shape of a large bird and it seemed to be struggling. It was much too large to be a raven so I decided to investigate further.

"I strapped on my snowshoes and with a rabbit snare and stick to hold this bird away I went to help him. When I got to him I was afraid that he might decide to bite me. I snared his head but while I was busy doing this he got me by the hand with the claws from both feet. My woolen gloves were no protection I can assure you. My next thought was, what do I do now in this predicament? With my free hand I took the stick and put it next to his feet. He removed his claws from my hand (which really hurt and was bleeding) and sank his claws into the stick instead. Then, with my hand that was not wounded I grabbed both his feet above the claws, and held him upside down while I attempted to free his wing from the barbed wire. . . .

"At this stage of the game it would be safe to say that my heart was beating about as fast as it could. I didn't want to injure the owl any more than he was, but it was necessary to pull his wing free of the wire. Finally I did free him and then turned him away from me, and he fluttered away about 10 feet. He then turned around and looked at me. I turned around and walked home to nurse my hand.

"I got in touch with the local conservation officer who captured the owl the following day. I learned from the officer that the owl had followed me most of the way home. Neighbors tell me that the owl had been in this area for the past two weeks and had no fear of buildings, houses etc. . . . You may wish to note that my rescue of the Great Gray Owl was an ordeal for both of us, for I am 70 years of age."

To gain information on Great Gray Owl population size, movements, sex and age ratios, and other biological data, we attempted to capture every bird we could find. Most were caught in winter when they were conspicuous and responsive. Operating under appropriate scientific permits, during the past twelve years we captured 171 full-grown adults and banded 49 nestling or fledgling birds—a total of 220. The figure astounds me; six years ago I would never have believed that we would reach that number. (The first Great Gray Owl ever banded in North America was captured only thirty-two years ago, in January 1947, near Toronto, by Gordon Lambert.)

From 1968 to 1973 inclusive, we banded only seven grown birds, but from 1974 to the end of June 1978 we banded sixty-nine. In the winter of 1978-79 we banded an unprecedented eighty-eight owls. Of the forty-nine young banded, forty-five were banded from summer 1974 to June 30, 1979. In less than eight months, from December 2, 1978, to July 8, 1979, we banded 110 birds (all in southeastern Manitoba), thus doubling our total. In the winter of 1979-80, an additional fifty birds were banded.

Our success in more recent years was due to the presence of large numbers of birds, improved capture techniques, and a greater effort. For example, in the winter of 1978-79, Herb Copland and I were in the field every weekend from November 26 to April 16, traveling as much as five hundred miles in a day. That winter was one of the longest and coldest ever recorded for Manitoba. On exceptional days we were able to band four to six adult owls. The length of time it took us to capture one varied from a few minutes to two hours or more. Owls were taken at all times of day, from earliest light to after dark, with a few unsuccessful attempts made at night. Weather conditions varied from dense fog (in mid-April), rain and snow, to bright sunlight. Generally, more birds were seen on calm, dark, cloudy days, often during a light snowfall. Early morning and late evening were also prime times. On windy days owls usually were difficult to find.

It took us at least thirty minutes to process a bird. That was the time spent from the moment of arrival back at the car to the release of the owl, including banding, measuring or describing twenty or more features, and recording in detail the state of molt. We also spray-painted the tips of the tail feathers twice, drying the feathers separately under the car heater both times (and, incidentally, leaving smears of paint on various parts of the car). We carefully avoided getting paint on the undertail coverts.

By painting the tail feathers (red, yellow, or green) we could tell which birds we had already banded, making it possible to identify banded and unbanded birds in a winter population. The ratio of marked to unmarked birds enabled us to estimate the numbers of birds in an area. Unfortunately, local wildlife photographers found our painted birds less appealing. Painting the tail is a temporary marking method. By June or July the paint will have faded or the tail feathers will have been renewed. It didn't seem to have any effect on the behavior of the birds, and more than one tail-painted bird was later found at a nest. The aluminum, numbered leg band, which we put on each bird, is a permanent means of identifying individuals, but the bird has to be captured (or found dead) for the band number to be read. A few breeding females, captured at the nest at the time we banded their young, were marked with brightly colored plasticized-nylon wing tags, one-inch-wide strips fastened in a loop around the base of each wing. It would take birds an hour or two to get used to the tag, but eventually they preened the tags into suitable position and thereafter bore them with little effort or signs of annoyance. These tags, which had identifying marks on the end, made it possible to follow the movements of individual birds from summer through winter.

They were sometimes retained for a year or more. I always felt a little reluctant to attach tags to birds. Obviously, it's a slight hindrance. But we've watched them raise their families successfully, apparently undeterred by the bright ribbons. In January and February the sight of a bird bearing a colored tag provides extra reassurance and unusual excitement, the additional information obtained from individual recognition of the owl making it all worthwhile.

We captured owls by a variety of techniques. For trapping birds in winter, we relied for the first several years on a standard bal-chatri trap, a small, wire-screen cage large enough to hold a live laboratory mouse, meadow vole, red squirrel, or House Sparrow. The cage is covered with upright, monofilament nylon slip-nooses set to catch the toes of the owl. Attracted to the live lure, an owl lands on the cage and is supposed to become en-tangled in the nooses. One noose pulled tight on a toe is enough to hold an owl; a weight attached to the trap prevents the bird from flying away. Sometimes this works well, but I have seen a trapped owl break a noose and escape. At other times I have watched helplessly and with disappointment while an owl repeatedly hopped about on the cage, trying to get at the lure, without getting caught.

Once, an owl hovered over a trap containing a red squirrel, inspecting the lure, and then flew away. On another occasion, a startled owl flew quickly away when a House Sparrow in a trap suddenly fluttered its wings. We soon decided that small rodents worked best. Laboratory mice were used most often. Although meadow voles are better able to withstand exposure to wind and low temperatures, we found them difficult to keep in captivity. Our most effective trap animal was the short-tailed shrew, hardier and even

more active than meadow voles, but not easy to find in winter.

Later, we used trapping methods that yielded better results, our most successful technique having been inspired by three published reports. In the first, Marilu L. Madura vividly described, more than twenty years ago in Wisconsin, how she lured a Red-tailed Hawk down from the sky by pulling a dead mouse some distance across a meadow with a length of fishline. Hiding in some nearby brush and hoping to lure the bird in for a photograph, she patiently waited for the hawk that daily hunted over the site. When it finally came into view she pulled the line, making the mouse jump out of the grass, whereupon the hawk swiftly spiralled down, following the mouse as she frantically continued to pull on the line. The hawk seized the mouse with one foot, when close to the observer, and then jerked the fishline from her grasp. "It was with a feeling of consternation that I saw with riveted gaze the long fishline, the captured mouse, and a few spears of dry grass in his talons trailing behind him."

That story had stayed with me all these years and was recalled upon reading a report by Daniel Brunton and Ronald Pittaway, who used the stuffed skin of a meadow vole towed by hand on a white string to lure Great Gray Owls wintering near Ottawa. The owls "would approach within an arm's length of the observers," they noted, to attack the moving skin. Brunton's field notes follow: "Got a bird to react to mouse-on-a-string; bird saw specimen on snow and immediately flew over to it, hovered briefly and dropped onto it, legs extended and wings folded over its back. When the specimen was pulled from the owl while it was still on the ground, the bird pursued it, taking 4 to 6 foot leaps across the snow, wings flapping, totally concentrated on the specimen. It chased it approximately 15 feet until I fell, then it grabbed it and attempted to fly off; a brief tug-of-war, then it released its grip and flew over to a small aspen from which it continued to stare at the specimen. The procedure was repeated and the owl attacked again when the specimen was very close to me—it apparently had no perception of my presence. The owl hit the specimen when it was about 2½ feet away, and only then it looked at me . . . with an expression that could only be described as shock and indignation! I attempted to catch the bird, but could only manage to grasp its wing

briefly. The owl flew off to a nearby sapling and stared intently back at me."

The mouse-on-a-string technique was adopted by Bob Fisher in October 1973 to study hunting behavior of a Hawk Owl in Alberta. To lure the owl, a white string was tied around the neck of a dead meadow vole which was then thrown out and retrieved by hand. "From 50 yards away," Fisher wrote, "I managed to attract the owl's attention to the vole by alternating quick movements with short pauses. The owl immediately flew to within 20 yards of me. Within 10 seconds it swooped down without a flap of its wings and, with both legs extended, landed on the back half of the vole. The owl, 8 feet in front of me, was holding its wings out as if balancing itself. I pulled on the string; at this movement the owl struck the vole's head with two sharp thrusts of its beak. Then it picked up the vole with its beak and flew into the forest."

When a large concentration of Great Grays appeared east of Winnipeg in the winter of 1974, I decided to try to build a better mouse. A reasonable facsimile of a fat meadow vole was made from a piece of wood covered with artificial fur from a hat; a piece of shoestring for a tail, an eyescrew at the other end—and there it was, an artificial mouse for fishing for owls! A bait-casting rod and level-winding reel with braided nylon line provided the means for throwing and retrieving the lure.

The first time I cast the lure at a Great Gray was on a bright, cold morning in February; it was minus 20 degrees Fahrenheit, but the air was still and the white landscape sparkled. We found our first owl perched in a frost-covered tree a hundred feet from the road, hunting intently. It paid no attention as I walked a few steps from the car, motor running, my son Woody and our springer spaniel looking out open windows. I cast across an open drift, and while the lure was still in midair the owl left its perch. With rapidly beating wings it came straight toward the lure, which now was sliding smoothly along on top of the snow. I reeled in line as fast as I could, but not fast enough— the owl swooped low, snatched up the lure, and turned away with its prize. I let some line run out, but finally had to jerk the lure free. This made the owl lurch in flight, but it turned and landed on a nearby tree. After a moment, while the owl watched closely, I made another short cast, letting the lure fall on the snow for a moment. Nothing happened. But as soon as I set the lure in motion, the owl came straight toward it, made a pass over it, turned on one wing, dropped and pounced. Again I had an owl on the end of my line, and once more reluctantly pulled the lure away. By then my fingers were numb with cold, though I was greatly enjoying myself.

Over the next two hours I cast the lure at four more owls with equal effect. The sight of the lemming-sized bait moving up and down snowdrifts like an over-sized, running vole, zigzagging between weed stalks as I teased it along, seemed to release a strong attack stimulus. I reeled fast or slow, watching the owl and trying to hold its attention by varying the lure's speed and action. One owl came down to the lure more than a dozen times, recklessly darting in as compulsively as a pike.

We used this technique for trapping owls for three months, leading a responding bird into a large throw-net laid flat on the snow and operated by a second person. Once an owl was sighted, the net was set out on a flat drift and the net operator crouched at one end of it, usually up to his waist in snow. The lure was then cast across the net and retrieved at a measured pace so that the owl would follow it and drop down onto or beside it in the middle of the net. A responsive owl would launch itself from its perch, fly rapidly toward us with continuous flapping, and then, for

the last several yards, approach in a smooth glide, eyes blinking rapidly as if to clear its vision as it neared the lure. At times the owl would veer off, but when things went right, the owl would suddenly be on the snow and in the net, flapping and kicking.

Since we were often casting for owls perched in trees beside a main highway, we sometimes slowed traffic, receiving curious looks from passing motorists. There were some disadvantages to the technique—it's almost impossible to use a rod and reel unless barehanded, and it's a miserable job trying to untangle a snarled line in subzero weather with an owl sitting nearby and one's companions impatiently waiting for the crucial cast. On those days I often had cold fingers and a short temper.

Though we had seen owls fly off after distant prey on the snow, we were still impressed when birds two hundred yards or more away from us responded to the lure the moment it began to move. On one occasion, when we were preparing to trap a distant owl, I stood at the back of the car, letting out some line to rewind on the reel to ensure a good cast. In the process, the lure fell to the road at my feet. At once the owl left its perch and flew rapidly toward us. When it swooped in at me, I whirled about, trying to keep the lure away from the bird, which flew around me, almost touching the car with it wings. Meanwhile, the rest of the crew looked on, stunned by the action. The owl flew off and, of course, couldn't be attracted again. Thereafter, though it seemed silly, I usually kept the lure in my hand or concealed at my side when approaching a bird.

All this while, another technique was available. Al Oeming had demonstrated a method on television in March 1974. He placed a live laboratory mouse on the snow, and when a Great Gray Owl flew in to get it, he captured it like a butterfly with a large fish-landing net. In late

March we tried his technique, using a nineteen-inch-diameter net with a two-and-one-half-foot-length handle—and it worked! One man with a net and a live mouse could capture a bird by himself. There were quick and immediate results, though not every bird responded. The main problem was the mice; at times in cold weather they wouldn't move enough, huddling in a ball, or suddenly darting off across the snow and out of reach of the net, so that a few owls got free meals.

It is an exciting game to play. Set the mouse loose and wait, motionless, watching the owl. Sometimes the least movement of the mouse, one turn, is enough to set an owl peering and craning; another move by the mouse and here comes the owl! Several rapid flaps of its wings, then a steady glide, bright yellow eyes staring fixedly, low across the field, straight in to the target. With the mouse less than four feet away and the approaching owl seeming to stare straight into one's eyes, it is almost unnerving. The bird looks huge when still far off, and one has to learn to wait for the critical moment—wait for the gliding owl to land beside the mouse and close its wings—then, quick, in one motion drop the landing net over it!

Great Gray Owls coming in to our live mice invariably landed close beside them rather than upon them, so the mice usually escaped injury. This manner of approaching prey was observed under more natural circumstances. One day, for example, an owl flew far out over an open field in pursuit of a vole scurrying on top of the snow. Gliding after it on set wings, the owl landed near the erratically moving vole, folded its wings for a second, then simply hopped onto its prey. Although a vole out on top of the snow is especially vulnerable, this sort of leisurely attack may relate to a bird's needs, a hungry owl probably making a more direct approach. Some owls picked mice off the snow without even pausing in flight.

Especially intriguing was the way in which Great Grays at times, with feet ex-

tended, slid in along the top of the snow behind the rapidly moving lure. By thus skidding on the surface of the snow they were able to catch the lure, and they probably take prey in this fashion when required. Though the birds are almost always in complete control of their movements, a hunting Great Gray Owl was seen taking a tumble late one winter evening. The owl swooped down upon a mouse running on the snow, reaching for it with both feet extended. Just as it struck the mouse it evidently caught a talon in the snow crust or on some hidden object, for the owl suddenly toppled forward with wings still extended, its momentum sending it somersaulting two or three times. But it held fast to its prey and finally flew off as if nothing unusual had happened.

A few years later we acquired a larger fish-landing net, using it to take owls pursuing the cast lure or coming in to a live mouse. It is oval-shaped, twenty-four inches wide and thirty-two inches long, with a fifty-eight-inch handle. This makes it feasible to net birds while they are still in the air, approaching, passing by, or even swerving away. It takes experience to judge when a bird can be safely netted and, because we didn't want to risk injuring a bird, sometimes we deliberately let one slip by. Once an owl lifted out of Herb's reach at the last moment, flew behind us and then returned, darting past me, stretching out one foot toward the lure that was lying on the handle of the net. I was speechless, and the bird flew right past Herb's head as it left. Herb was still motionless, waiting for the bird to return to its perch, to make another pass at the lure.

Even if the owl isn't captured, the sight of it sailing in at close range is impressive. When it hovers nearby or veers away, its flapping wings are noiseless, even when within arm's reach. Skimming by with feathers in immaculate order, it has a remarkably trim appearance. Only the flat, forward-directed face looks anom-

alous, at odds with the otherwise stream-lined form. What a contrast between this beautiful bird and the same struggling, disheveled creature in the net!

Working as a team, we followed a general pattern, first trying to attract an owl with the cast lure, often netting it directly. At other times the cast lure served to bring an owl closer to us so that we could try other methods. If a bird failed to come in on the cast lure, the person with the net would take a live mouse out of his pocket (where it was kept comfortable with a handwarmer) and place it on the snow, or, better, on a white cloth-covered board. A long period of trying to seduce the owl with a live mouse was sometimes necessary before the owl would fly down to be netted. If this didn't work we still had bal-chatri traps, and often dropped these on the edge of the road from the slowly moving car when trying to get a shy bird. In the winter of 1978–79 we obtained a Verbail trap, a neat device that supplemented the bal-chatri. Invented in the 1920s by biologist Vernon Bailey, the Verbail could be fastened onto a bal-chatri or attached to a pole set nearby as a perch for the owl. When an owl landed on top of the treadle, this triggered off a tightly flexed spring wire that would in turn quickly draw a cord noose about the bird's feet. We found it to be a safe and sure method of capturing Great Gray Owls. The trick was to get them to land on top of it. Now when we're out looking for owls we travel with a full load of gear: live mice in warm boxes, bal-chatris, the

Verbail, nets, casting rod and lure, and banding equipment. Upon sighting an owl there's a certain amount of scrambling to get things in hand, and more than once owls have quietly disappeared while we were getting ready.

I can recall numerous stories of adventure or misadventure in connection with capturing or trying to capture owls. We spent some long hours, for example, digging our vehicle out of snow-filled, hidden ditches. We also had problems with flat tires, barking dogs, curious motorists, birdwatchers eager to see the action, and snowmobilers.

One sunny day we stopped to try for an owl seen ahead of us, perched on a utility pole. We barely had time to get our equipment out when suddenly a snowmobiler appeared, speeding toward us along the line of poles, certain to frighten the owl away. We ran ahead to the edge of the road and I made a hasty cast while Herb was still getting himself in position with the net. The owl left the pole when the lure started moving, just as the snowmobiler reached the same pole. It was a race between the two; we could see both the owl gliding toward us and a spume of snow from the noisy machine coming up behind it. Despite the potential distraction, the owl kept right on course. Seconds after Herb netted it, the snowmobiler pulled up alongside us to see what we were doing.

Another day, spotting an owl hunting from a stump in an open field about a hundred yards from the edge of a highway,

we stopped and made a cast. As I started reeling in the lure, the owl leapt off its perch, flapped heavily several times, and headed directly toward us. Just as it set its wings in a glide, it was joined by a second bird, equally intent on the lure. Where the latter bird came from we had no idea; all we could do was marvel at the spectacle of two Great Gray Owls side by side, wing tips almost touching, round faces fixed on the moving lure, gliding rapidly toward us. Herb netted the nearest bird, the other swerved up and over us at the same time and settled in a nearby small tree, where we caught it a few minutes later.

Sometimes we captured Great Grays with a wire snare on the end of a long pole, thus taking a few winter birds and females at nests after the young were well grown. Capturing an owl with this technique can be an agonizing experience: trying to raise the delicate snare up through branches and twigs to the perched owl before it moves away, desperately manipulating it into position over the bird's head—all this, while the owl is moving its

Herb Copland is ready for action. Note the live mouse near the net.

Inch-long talons are a good reason for keeping a firm grip on the owl's feet as it is banded.

head about in annoyance each time the snare brushes against its feathers. One minute the bird is aloft, perched, balanced, magnificent, out of reach, staring downward or across the forest; then when the snare is pulled, the owl suddenly is brought down, wings flailing. One rushes forward to secure it, to keep it from hurting itself, to undo the snare, to restore some of the bird's lost dignity, rearranging its feathers and cradling it to bring it to a quiet state. The whole affair sounds appalling, but little harm is done; owing to an abundance of feathers on the neck, the wire seldom draws tight.

When a bird is trapped, by whatever means, one must control it, holding the feet tightly and always being watchful of the talons, gathering in the wings against the body. The talons, being long and sharp and quick to close, can produce painful punctures and scratches. An owl is insecure except in flight or when properly perched; the constant flexing of its toes when it is being handled is probably due to the bird's need to hold onto something, rather than aggressive behavior. Occasionally, an individual will snap its bill and try to bite. Such birds, recorded as "a biter and struggler," frequently nipped at me with their bills and seldom stopped struggling, making it difficult to carry on our work. These were more often adult females, which are generally more aggressive in nature than males; but occasionally an adult male or an immature bird of either sex would show similar behavior. I was impressed by the strength of their legs, which have a heavy musculature. At times, when the bird shoved its feet forward, or tried to, I had to exert considerable force to keep it in position against my body.

Once held properly, legs grasped firmly in one hand, wings tucked in and the body embraced and upright against one's chest, most Great Gray Owls are relatively tractable. They submit to being stroked, and indeed seem to enjoy having their "ears" scratched just as a cat or dog does. Gentle probing with a finger deep into the feathers behind the ear opening sometimes causes them to tilt their heads sideways, suggesting a favorable response to grooming, a remarkable behavior for a freshly captured wild animal. Most of the owls I've handled have been surprisingly docile. It's difficult to resist caressing and nuzzling one of these beautiful, warm, soft-plumaged birds. Though perhaps a sentimental gesture, burying my nose deep in the side of the big feathered head gives me pleasure. The smell is of warm feathers, a pleasant scent.

Trapping and handling a bird didn't seem to have much lasting effect. Sometimes we watched birds for fairly long periods after they were released, and generally their behavior appeared normal. One marked bird, taken in the Verbail trap, two weeks later responded strongly to the cast lure, once even picking it up and flying away with it. One owl, captured via the cast lure and net technique, pursued the same lure as if it had never seen it before, only forty minutes after being released. In this case I tested the bird only because she stayed near us and kept right on hunting; it was evidently a hungry owl.

I suspect it is mostly hunger that drives Great Gray Owls to respond to our lures, making them almost totally ignore us in their urge to take prey. A resident of The Pas, John Donald, told me that on several occasions when he encountered Great Gray Owls, to amuse his children he threw a mitten onto the snow, bringing the owl down close. Another friend, less acquainted with this species, tossed his wallet out the car window late one winter evening to see what would happen. He told me he was surprised to see how close the bird came; it actually landed on the wallet for a brief moment. I told him he was lucky the bird didn't carry it away! Sounds, as well as objects, attract them. Once, in good light, while we stood by our car, squeaking to draw the attention of a Great Gray Owl to a mouse in a balchatri trap, a second bird appeared. Evidently attracted by the sound, it flew toward us, suddenly stopped short and pounced on a lump of brown ice in the center of the highway. It sat for a few seconds foolishly looking at its mistaken prey before flying away.

Winter banding draws to a close in late March or mid-April when, with the melting of snow, small rodents are more readily available, and owls have returned to distant nesting grounds, or are busily engaged at nest sites back in the woods. The number of owls to be found out in the open rapidly decreases, it becomes increasingly difficult to approach those that one does find, and they become much less responsive. Suddenly, winter is over.

5

An Elusive Bird

By what powerful alchemy have the northern coniferous forest and its inhabitants been brought to the present artful arrangement? By what magic do snowshoe hares suddenly cover the forest floor, providing a rich bounty that moves a hundred systems, and then as suddenly disappear, leaving hungry predators desperately searching for food, running and flying, fleeing to far places, and dying?

Perhaps the owl knows. Itself a creature of bog and forest, the Great Gray Owl has shared in the slow, cold death and eventual rebirth of northern woodlands. Watching the silent struggle of plants and animals moving northward after the crushing ice masses re-shaped the land, the owl became part of the fragile network, adjusting to the ebb and rise of a tide of small rodents, themselves responding to subtle forces. A bird of mystery, the Great Gray Owl bears in its aloofness some of the remoteness of the vast northland; its plumage the color of lichens and weathered wood; its soft hooting, part of the wind.

Hare and lynx, caribou and wolf, mouse and owl—in no other region is there such a precarious arrangement of cause and effect. Something tips in the balance and a million conifers produce a burden of cones, feeding nuthatches, crossbills, squirrels, voles, and mice, and these in turn are food for predators, furbearers, animals important to man. Another season, and the failure of the cone crop sends waves of birds far outside their normal range.

In the balance of things, an owl, a mouse, a single plant entwined in the decayed roots of a toppled spruce, may be part of the answer. The explorer, the scientist, the poet, pondering these problems, must look everywhere, must enquire of all the creatures that live in these woods—the woods of the Great Gray Owl.

British explorers during the North American fur trade era discovered both the Great Gray Owl and its nest. The species was described first by John R. Forster in 1772 on the basis of a specimen sent to England in 1771 by Hudson Bay Company factor and naturalist Andrew Graham. At the time, Graham was at Severn (then Fort Severn or Severn House), which is at the mouth of the Severn River on the west coast of Hudson Bay in northwestern Ontario, about seventy miles from the Manitoba-Ontario boundary. Graham received many bird skins already "stuffed and dried" by Indians and obtained inland, but it is not clear how the first Great Gray Owl specimen seen by any interested white man came into his possession. That he saw other Great Gray Owls, and in the flesh if not alive, is clear from his remarks that "some only weigh two pounds one quarter, others three pounds."

Fifty-four years later the first nest known to science was found by Sir John Richardson at Great Bear Lake. The indefatigable Richardson reported: "On the 23rd of May [1826], I discovered a nest of this Owl, built on the top of a lofty balsam-poplar, of sticks, and lined with feathers. It contained three young, which were covered with a whitish down. We got them by felling the tree, which was remarkably thick; and whilst this operation was going on, the two parent birds flew in circles round the objects of their cares, keeping, however, so high in the air as to be out of gunshot: they did not appear to be dazzled by the light." Richardson must have been intrigued by the owlets, which survived the fall, for instead of turning them into scientific study skins he kept them alive for two months, no mean feat under the conditions of their expedition. The first behavioral observation of young of the species is his brief comment that "they had the habit, common to other Owls, of throwing themselves back and making a loud snapping noise with their bills, when any one entered the room in which they were kept." Rather laconically, he adds that after keeping them that long "they made their escape."

Richardson and William Swainson (the latter an ornithologist who collaborated with the physician-naturalist on their joint 1831 publication) gave a remarkably good account of the distribution of the Great Gray Owl in Canada, especially considering the paucity of information available at the time. They noted that the species "is by no means a rare bird in the fur-countries, being an inhabitant of all the woody districts lying between Lake Superior and latitudes 67° or 68°, and between Hudson's Bay and the Pacific. It is common on the borders of Great Bear Lake; and there and in the higher parallels of latitude it must pursue its prey, during the summer months, by daylight."

The Great Gray Owl (*Strix nebulosa*) occupies a vast circumpolar range, being resident across the coniferous forest belt of Eurasia and western North America at both low and high elevations. The Eurasian subspecies (*Strix nebulosa lapponica*), paler and more strongly streaked than its North American counterpart, resides in northern Norway, Sweden, Finland, and the Soviet Union. Initially thought to be a separate species, it was long known as the Lapland Owl or Lapp Owl. In Russia it has been called the Wood Owl, Bearded Night Owl, or Bearded Owl, the last two names owing to the small patch of black feathers beneath its "chin" or bill. When common names for subspecies were in vogue, this race was identified as the Siberian Great Gray Owl. The North American subspecies (*Strix nebulosa nebulosa*) has been known in the past as the Cinereous Owl, Great Cinereous Owl and Sooty Owl—references to its grayish-brown color. It has also been called the Speckled Owl, the Spruce Owl, and the Spectral Owl. Edward H. Forbush, speaking of the former scientific name of the species, noted: "*Scotiaptex nebulosa*, the name which systematists have given the Great Gray Owl, certainly is descriptive of this bird. Freely translated it runs thus—'The gray eagle-owl of darkness.'"

In fact not a bird of darkness, but a bird of light, the Great Gray Owl is distinct among its kind, being the only species among the eleven in the genus *Strix* that is not primarily nocturnal. The noticeably small eyes of Great Grays are undoubtedly an adaptation for daylight hunting, a feature evolved during the origin of the species in the circumpolar Arctic region long before the Ice Age. It is, incidentally, the only species of the genus that occurs in both the Old and New Worlds. Numerous aspects of form and behavior, achieved through a long period of time in forested regions in extreme northern latitudes, are a heritage carried by both geographic races. Though divided into two separate populations, North American and Eurasian birds have retained almost all features in common, hence, for the most part, can be treated as one.

Though it occurs northward to the northern limit of dense evergreen forests on both continents, the Great Gray Owl's range in Europe and western North America extends far southward. Its known North American breeding range runs from central Alaska and Canada south in the western mountains to central California, northern Idaho, western Wyoming and Montana, extreme northwestern Minnesota, and south-central Ontario. There is an apparent extra-limital nesting record for extreme northwestern Wisconsin. In Canada, the heart of its North American breeding range, it breeds in most of British Columbia, northern and central Alberta, northern Saskatchewan, all of Manitoba except the extreme northern and southwestern parts, and Ontario west of James Bay; though it likely breeds east of James Bay and into Quebec, there are few summer records for that large region.

Great Gray Owls occur across a large and varied region on this continent, ranging from stunted, transition forest in the Hudson Bay Lowlands to subalpine and montane forests from Alaska to California and Wyoming. Birds occasionally venturing out on the tundra undoubtedly have feasted on lemmings; others have roamed quietly on the edge of meadows above timberline at high altitudes. But it is with the northernmost forest cover that these birds are most closely associated.

Like many other owls, the Great Gray lays its eggs in nests built by other species, such as crows, ravens, and various hawks. Accordingly, its nests naturally vary considerably in height, shape, durability, and in the habitat in which they occur. In Alberta their preferred nesting habitat is considered to be stands of mature poplar adjacent to muskeg country. Islands of black poplar or aspen poplar amid a sea of spruce and pine are probably attractive nesting places for birds that build large, stick nests. The dominant tree species over much of the northern range is black spruce. And even on wintering grounds, sometimes miles from known nesting range, black spruce-tamarack forests are seldom far away. There also is good evidence that the deciduous tamarack or larch, which often accompanies spruce, occurring as islands within spruce stands, along wet margins or as extensive stands, may be especially important as breeding habitat.

Considered common in eastern Siberia, the Great Gray Owl is scarce in Europe and much of its North American range. Still, these owls may be more abundant than is generally believed. Scandinavian workers have amassed a great deal of information on the species, having recorded more than one hundred and thirty nests. According to Heimo Mikkola, a Finnish ornithologist who has long studied the species, the most dense concentration of breeding Great Grays has been observed in northern Finland.

Despite its large range in North America, only a little more than a hundred

North American breeding range of the Great Gray Owl. In winter, owls sometimes wander outside the breeding range. Some winters large incursions are observed in the hatched area. Arrows show areas of suspected breeding.

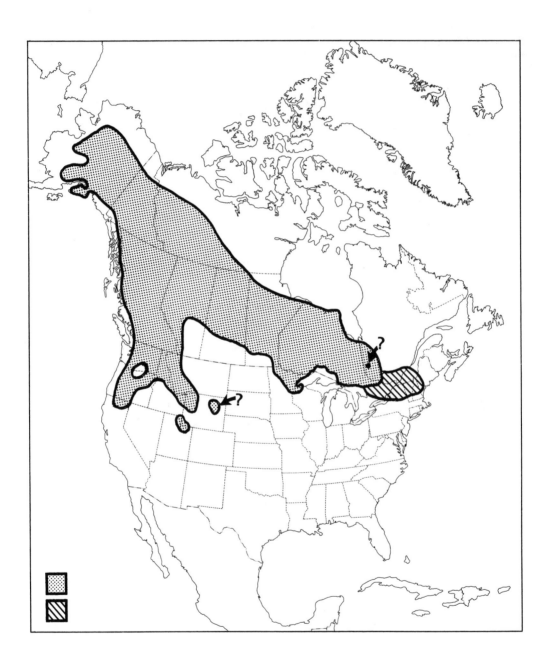

Great Gray Owl breeding distribution is within or close to the boundaries of the Boreal Forest Zone.

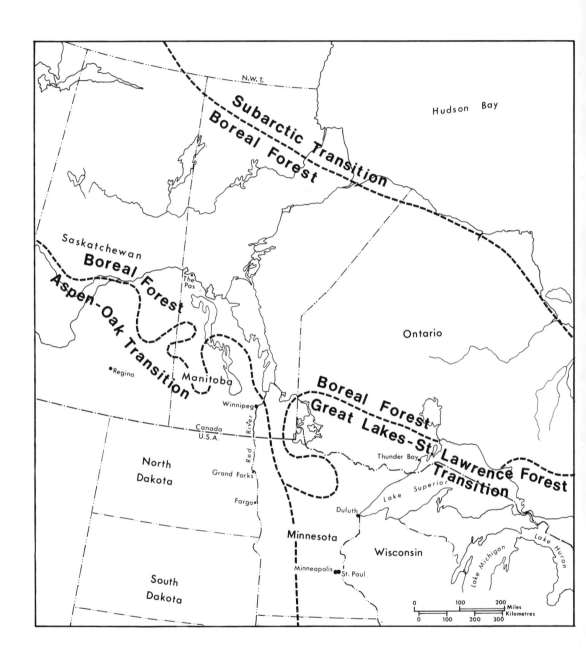

nests were found in the 150 years after Richardson's discovery of a nest at Great Bear Lake. Sets of eggs—egg clutches—in museums provide the largest number of nest records. Early naturalists took the eggs from almost every nest they discovered, but this aspect of scientific collecting would have had little effect on the overall population. The majority of the nests were found in Canada, especially in Alberta.

Owing to its dependence on small mammals for food, this species suffers severely when its prey declines, at times undergoing starvation or making lengthy migrations into southern Europe. Thus, its numbers fluctuate according to local conditions, making it difficult to arrive at overall population estimates. Similar conditions operate to some extent in North America, owls occasionally appearing in numbers in southeastern Canada and adjacent United States.

How many Great Gray Owls are there in North America? The range of the species is so large and there is so little information available regarding its density that it is difficult to estimate their abundance. Judging by our experience in Manitoba and Minnesota, I believe that there may be upward of fifty thousand. Many people will think this figure is too high for a species considered rare or uncommon. But we have learned how secretive they can be when nesting, how seldom seen except at the nest site. We have seen concentrations of winter birds of fifty or more in a relatively small area, and our evidence suggests that these are mostly local birds, from good breeding habitat within thirty to fifty miles. Much remains to be learned about the species, not the least of which is population density and abundance.

Ready wanderers, quick to leave nesting grounds when prey is scarce, and likely to nest elsewhere should they find prey and

In earlier times, eggs from most Great Gray Owl nests that were discovered were taken for museum collections.

suitable nest sites, there is evidence that Great Gray Owls have an attachment to their original breeding sites, or at least the general area. Two marked females that bred successfully in Manitoba in 1978 were seen on numerous occasions during the following winter within a mile or two of their nest sites. In Sweden, as reported by Wahlstedt, three adult females banded at nests in 1973 used the same nests the following year! Their habit of remaining on the breeding grounds in years of poor food supply and simply not breeding shows an adaptability to declining prey species as well as a means for sedentary existence. Occasional irruptions may result from a combination of years of good reproductive success followed by abrupt prey declines. Ecologist Charles S. Elton, it should be noted, included the Great Gray Owl as a member of several boreal forest species exhibiting this characteristic pattern.

Writing in 1927, Forbush gave an over-simplified explanation of the appearances of Great Grays in the New England states: "When the northern forests fail to produce cones for winter food for small arboreal birds; when deep snows cover the runways of mice, and grasses and weeds that feed ground-birds and when bush rabbits and ptarmigan are scarce in the northern wilderness; then we may expect an unusual invasion of Great Gray Owls."

High populations of owls, scarcity of food due to low numbers of small mammals and other prey species, icy crusts, or unusually deep snow may account for appearances and concentrations of owls within the breeding range as well as in adjacent areas. Occurrences of owls hundreds of miles beyond their normal range, however, are less easy to understand. What compels them onward, flying slowly over open terrain, across alien country? Is it hunger alone? Or do they have an inherent urge to move, released by some of the factors mentioned above, that drives them outward from their breeding grounds? Is there, perhaps, some biological advantage to this movement that at times leads them astray, into inhospitable areas, into cities and towns, where many eventually perish?

One of our young birds, banded in May 1976 as a nestling about fifty miles east of Winnipeg, was found dead on a roadside in extreme southeastern Minnesota, about twelve miles from the Iowa border. That is about four hundred and sixty-eight miles in a straight line from the nest site. Presumably the bird hadn't left the natal area until September, for until then it should have been a weak flier. Douglas Butler, a motorist who found the remains of the bird in mid-March 1977, wrote me that he thought it had been dead for three to four weeks. In five months or less, then, the young owl made that extended journey. On the other hand, another young owl, banded in the nest by us in 1978, was struck by a car in mid-October of that year, less than a mile from the nest site.

In the winter of 1978-79 unprecedented numbers of Great Gray Owls appeared in southern Ontario and Quebec. I was told that at the peak in January and early February there were about forty birds in the Toronto vicinity, and an equal number near Kingston on Amherst Island (where nine were seen in one tree!), and eighteen or so on the adjacent mainland. About fifty were reported in the Ottawa vicinity, where, over the course of the winter, many were shot or starved to death. During that same period, numerous sightings were made in upper New York State and New England. That same winter, Great Gray Owls were seen in abundance in southeastern Manitoba, with perhaps a hundred birds occurring in an area described by a circle with a diameter of forty miles, centering some seventy miles northeast of Winnipeg. From December through April, Herb Copland and I captured and banded eighty-eight owls in that area. Large numbers had been observed in

a portion of that area in the winter of 1973-74, when we trapped fourteen birds, and again in the winter of 1977-78, when we took thirty.

Birds appearing in winter far from known breeding range, such as those in New York and the New England states, are clearly emigrants, displaced birds. Their origin is unknown, but there is little doubt that they are far from home. The appearance of the owls in winter in southeastern Manitoba is less unexpected because this area is within their breeding range. Active nests over several years, occasional recaptures, and especially sightings of color-tagged females that bred successfully in the area emphasize the point that the wintering population east of Winnipeg consists of both resident and nonresident birds.

Although the estimated numbers present in winters of high populations in Manitoba are impressive, I think that these birds can be accounted for by movement of owls from nearby breeding grounds. Areas of concentration for these birds were ideal hunting sites, consisting of open, grassy fields adjacent to woods. A high meadow vole population in 1978-79 undoubtedly contributed to the unusual number of owls. The ratio of resident to nonresident birds is unknown, but nonresidents could be coming from adjacent breeding habitat that stretches for hundreds of miles. So there is little reason to think that Manitoba birds are coming any great distance.

Birds appearing in Duluth and southern Ontario and Quebec could be coming from not-too-distant breeding grounds, for

Not at all amused, a captive bird glares at its captors. Though owl "faces" are less mobile and expressive than those of mammals, because the former lack the complex facial musculature, some range of expression does exist.

suitable habitat lies not far from these areas. What is not known is the population density of Great Gray Owls on those more remote breeding grounds, let alone in our more accessible study areas. Birds may be coming in some cases from great distances, but one need not necessarily look too far in northern Canada for a source of birds appearing in southern Canada and adjacent United States.

Conspicuous appearances of Great Grays during periods of emigration (related to over-abundance or food shortages or both) may lead to misinterpretation of population size. Actual populations may be much higher, or lower, than estimated on the basis of winter appearances. This species can occur regularly without being particularly obtrusive. Like most owls, they are generally retiring, keeping to remote or dense woods and avoiding man. Except at active nests or during critical winter periods when they are forced to hunt during daylight hours, their presence in an area may go unnoticed.

There is no reason to believe, on the other hand, that Great Grays occur uniformly throughout their range. Numerous water bodies, vast stretches of open bogs and stunted trees to the north, and even-aged, dense stands of spruce and pine elsewhere are likely devoid of resident birds. Moreover, in large regions of apparently ideal habitat there are few summer or winter records. The species likely varies locally in abundance, increasing and decreasing from time to time with rodent population fluctuations and other limiting factors. Changes in habitat through extensive clear-cutting of trees, for example, or extensive forest fires, undoubtedly also affect its numbers and distribution. Archibald Henderson suggested that in Alberta the species flourished during low density populations of other raptors, an abundance of vacant nests providing maximum opportunity for selection of suitable sites. Great Gray Owls did well when raptors such as Great Horned Owls, Goshawks,

and Red-tailed Hawks diminished, following declines in numbers of snowshoe hares and grouse, the prey species on which they most depend. It must be presumed, though, that there was a fair supply of small rodents in those areas where Great Grays nested.

Despite many more observers in much of its North American range, there has not been a corresponding increase in observations of this species. Though there is evidence of recent nesting in Saskatchewan, the last recorded Great Gray Owl nest was found there in 1949. This, despite the fact that C. Stuart Houston, M.D., an enthusiastic birder by avocation, has had a wide network of cooperators searching methodically across the province for nesting raptors since 1958. Up to 1979 Dr. Houston had banded an astonishing 2,885 nestling or fledgling Great Horned Owls (his specialty) at 1,248 nests. The scarcity of breeding Great Gray Owls and relatively few winter records for Saskatchewan suggest that the population in that province is low compared to Manitoba. At present Saskatchewan has far less tamarack-bog habitat than Manitoba; this may be the reason for the striking difference in population levels in these regions.

More than three dozen nests have been found in Alberta, yet this species has been considered scarce and "even close to extermination" by some Alberta ornithologists. Henderson found thirteen nests between 1913 and 1922 near his home at Belvedere (collecting all the eggs in nearly every case!). For the next thirty years, however, he found none. From 1950 to 1955 Al Oeming and several companions "travelled 36,000 miles over every conceivable type of terrain and using every imaginable means of navigation. . . . Thousands of trappers, loggers, Indians and other woodspeople were interviewed. . . ." Eventually two nests were discovered. Oeming concluded that the Great Gray Owl in Alberta was a vanishing species, though writing in 1955:

A male owl feeds a female on a curved bough in a tamarack forest. Sometime between January and April, as part of courtship behavior, a male brings food to a female for the first time, thereby establishing a close relationship with her. He continues to feed her during courtship, egg laying, incubation, and the development of the nestlings—who must also be supplied with prey by the male.

The female has taken the mouse from the male and is about to gulp it down. From this moment on, the pair bond is assured.

"Recently the Alberta Government passed
an Act protecting all the hawks and owls
in the province. In such protection rests
the Great Gray Owl's last chance of survival. Education of the public, strict ob-
servance of the new law, and preservation
of suitable nesting areas may yet ensure
the continued existence of this rare, beautiful and beneficial owl." Oeming's fore-
cast now appears reasonable, for between
1970 and 1974, north and northwest of
Edmonton, two dedicated birders, Edgar T.
Jones and Robert E. Gehlert, found nine
Great Gray nests.

The discovery of twenty-six Great Gray
Owl nests, and good evidence for several
other recent nestings, in a small region of
Manitoba and adjacent Minnesota from
1970 to 1979 shows that the species is
doing well in this area. This is not to say
that the species is not rare. By comparison
with many other birds, Great Gray Owls
are indeed uncommon, but perhaps no
more so than other northern coniferous-
forest-dwelling raptors such as Hawk
Owls and Boreal Owls.

6

The Species—A Closer Look

Standing on a road in Great Gray Owl country late on a cold, damp April night we throw back our parka hoods and listen. Across the starlit bog a chill sits on all the black spruce huddled shoulder to shoulder, their irregular heavy heads just perceptible on the horizon. It is still. We wait and wait, and then, there! a faint, soft, almost booming sound. A long series of regularly spaced hoots, all on the same note, then speeding up while dropping in volume, leaving us uncertain when the last note has sounded. In a moment, again, the distant call, an emphatic "Hoo-hoo-hoo-hoo," unhurried and deliberate, at the close faintly echoing over the bog. From another direction comes a reply, at first soft, mellow, each note carefully drawn, a decisive message from a second owl.

It is remarkably quiet . . . it is too early for frogs, and apart from a distant Great Horned Owl no other birds are active. We shuffle about, speaking quietly, staring out into the night as if we thought we could see them, listening for another call. Then it comes, much closer, and now each note is heavier, somehow intense, perhaps huskier or more rasping than before. We sense a greater meaning in the calls, now coming one right after the other, the two owls evidently responding to each other, declaring their territorial boundaries. "Hoo-hoo-hoo-hoo!" exclaims each bird in turn, and on what thread of meaning, what fine tuning, what peculiar vibrancy of the calls their interrelationship revolves we do not know.

For us, listening in the night has a dreamlike quality; we stand stiffly hunched, envisioning owls silently flying from perch to perch, following each nuance of sound in each other's calls. When the calls finally cease, a calm stillness falls upon us. Having found what we sought, we stamp our feet, speak softly, and nod agreeably, then hurry to the warm confines of the car, on to the next listening post.

Life on the forest floor provides a food base for Great Gray Owls. The red-backed vole is an important prey species.

Below: Newly hatched chicks rest their heads on a remaining egg. Considering the size of Great Gray Owls, the eggs are surprisingly small—little more than two inches long and less than that in width—not even as large as a hen's egg.

A clutch of four eggs is about average for Great Gray Owls, but in years when prey species abound, the female may lay more. While most owl eggs are round, those of Great Grays are ovoid or conical.

"Strix capite laevi, corpore fusco, albido undulatim striato, remige sexto longiore, apice nigricante"—so begins John Forster's Latin description of the Great Gray Owl, published in 1772, more than two centuries ago. A more informal and appealing description was given in 1960 by a Saskatchewan farmer, Clifford Law, whose land lay adjacent to Great Gray breeding grounds: "The most conspicuous features of the Great Gray Owl are its large round head and its very dark feathers. The width of the owl's head would be between five and six inches at the base. Because of the thick head feathers, the face looks flat and sunken." The large, round head and circular facial disc are features characteristic of the genus.

Up to thirty inches in length, with a tail a foot or more long, and a wingspan up to five feet, the Great Gray is a large bird. As Richardson noted: "the *tail* is wedge-shaped, consisting of twelve feathers, of which the outer ones are more than two inches shorter than the middle ones: it is very concave below."

A taxidermist, after looking over a specimen killed at Wickford, Rhode Island, on March 25, 1883, concluded: "Taken all in all, it is the most bird for the least substance we ever examined." This apt statement has since been repeated almost verbatim by several authors. Arthur C. Bent wrote that "in bodily bulk it is exceeded by the snowy and great horned owls and is but little larger than the barred owl; its long wings and tail, its large, round head, and its long fluffy plumage make it seem much larger than it really is." Great Grays weigh roughly two to three pounds, females generally being heavier than males and occasionally weighing up to four pounds. Body weights also vary with a bird's condition, emaciated individuals falling as low as three-quarters of a pound.

In owls of nearly all species, females are larger than males, but the sexes are otherwise similar in appearance. Although some observers have stated that female

Great Grays are darker than males, there is much individual variation, pale and dark birds of both sexes being known. When a pair is seen together, the size difference between the sexes is readily apparent, but single birds are difficult to identify. Even in the hand, though there is a size difference and some as yet undefined facial features that help differentiate the sexes, their measurements overlap, and sexes cannot always be identified with certainty. Throughout winter, because of long exposure to sunlight and abrasive forces, the feathers of older birds are usually brownish or beige in color, in contrast to the truer gray color of younger birds in fresh plumage. This is particularly noticeable in the tail, which may be badly worn at the tip, and in flight feathers of the wings. The worn, faded tail feathers of an adult female, who may have spent much of the summer exposed on a nest, may appear markedly paler than the rest of her plumage, standing out even at a distance. Primary and secondary feathers are often lighter and browner than the rest of the plumage; if viewed with binoculars (or in a photograph), one may discern new, dark feathers among the old. Even in summer, old and new flight feathers may be apparent.

After recovering a known-age, banded young owl, and then handling a large number of birds in the winter of 1978–79, we became aware of plumage features whereby birds hatched in one season could be separated from older birds from late summer through April. Young birds generally have grayer or darker plumage; although varying individually, their plumage appears overall as one color. Their primary and secondary feathers and tail feathers are alike in age and color. On this basis, along with additional features, subadult owls can be recognized almost as soon as captured. Of the eighty-eight birds captured in the winter of 1978–79, roughly one-third were identified as young from the previous summer.

We recorded the appearance of each

flight feather in both wings and the tail in more than a hundred Great Gray Owls. This large body of data has yet to be analyzed. At present, I can say that the molt pattern is complex and not fully understood!

Because birds lack the complex facial musculature of mammals, their "faces" are less mobile and hence less expressive. Nevertheless, some facial expression is possible. In owls, especially, with forward-facing eyes and unusual development of certain facial feathers, a considerable range of expression is achieved. There is a vast difference between an owl peering sleepily through half-closed eyelids and one staring menacingly with fully open, round eyes. Even changes in the size of the pupil, notable in owls because of an almost instant response to changes in light level, occur in different moods.

Owls typically have a foreshortened appearance, as if the face had been flattened to bring the eyes onto one plane, thus achieving binocular vision. Completing the characteristic owl face is a circle of feathers surrounding the eyes. The latter aspect is related to development of acute hearing. Nearly all birds have specialized feathers called auriculars or ear coverts on the sides of the head behind the eyes. The stiff coverts protect the opening to the inner ear while offering minimal resistance to sound waves. In owls, where hunting by sound is a particular specialty, extensive and enlarged ear coverts, supported by a fleshy flap, are fanned out around the eyes. Supporting this auricular flap and forming a semicircular trough nearly surrounding each ear opening is a dense wall of stiff feathers with flattened quills. The disc is a sound-gathering device, contributing to the remarkable hearing ability of owls.

Hudson Bay factor Andrew Graham astutely commented as far back as 1772 on the peculiar structure of the feathers covering the external ear openings in the Great Gray Owl: "In examining the external ear which is very large I observed a

As this late evening silhouette of a bird
on a fence post shows, the Great Gray
Owl's white "chin stripes" are visible
even in poor light.

An aerial display at twilight. With the
sun at tree level, an owl glides into the
picture.

Great Gray Owls, which typically use stick nests built by hawks, crows, ravens, and other species, may begin hunting for nest sites as early as mid-February. The male plays an important role in finding a suitable nest, but the female probably makes the final choice.

range of short brown feathers. All the other feathers within the circle are grey with obscure bars of black, stiff and very thinly furnished with webs similar to hair by the peculiar direction of providence, for without this provision the perception of sounds would be very difficult in a bird so remarkably full of plumage."

A greatly enlarged facial disc, extending far above the top of the cranium, partly accounts for the large head of the Great Gray. The ear coverts are concealed by softer feathers radiating out from the eyes and marked by six or more brown concentric rings on a gray background. The disc forms a nearly complete circle, the center of which lies midway between the eyes. Each half of the facial disc is slightly concave and angled backward. In the Great Gray, especially when relaxed or dozing, the upper half of the disc may be moved forward over the eyes, giving a heavy-browed effect. In this position, with lower, pale gray-colored eyelids raised in sleeping attitude, the eyes seem deeply set within the owl's head.

The color of the bill of grown birds varies in puzzling fashion from ivory to pale olive green to bright yellow. Olive green is the color most often recorded, both in summer and winter. At first I assumed that an increasing amount of yellow pigment indicated advancing reproductive condition. Some January birds had vivid yellow bills (retained in some study skins). I changed my mind, however, after noting that birds with young had bills that were pale olive green with a marked ochre-colored cere or base and ochre-colored rictus (fleshy edge of inner bill). The ochre color, so prominent in breeding females, was generally not noted in winter birds. Some birds in winter had a bill that was pale olive green or yellowish, with an ivory tip, and a dark olive green or blackish base! Clearly, there is more to be learned about bill color in this species.

Rictal bristles, modified feathers at the base of the bill, are found in many species. They are especially large and prominent in owls, extending up and between the eyes. In Great Grays, the rictal bristles appear as two opposite-facing crescents partly surrounding the eyes and usually concealing all but the tip of the bill. Because these feathers are light colored or even white in this species, they stand out boldly and are a distinctive part of the facial plumage. When an owl is feeding or preening, the feathers of the lower half of these white crescents are usually raised, exposing the entire bill. This frees the bill for action and also helps to keep adjacent feathers from getting soiled. During aggressive situations, the bristles about the bill are fully erected, giving the bird a more fearsome appearance.

In all birds the bill acts as a substitute in carrying out tasks rendered with forelimbs in many animals, including nest building, grooming, handling food, and manipulating eggs and young. The delicacy with which such tasks are performed serves to remind us of the numerous functions of the bill. An owl's bill is thus more than a device for seizing prey. In the Great Gray, prominent tactile bristles surround the bill and eyes, doubtless assisting the bird in a wide range of activities, much like the whiskers of a cat. Bending far forward to turn her eggs or to check the conditions of nestlings, or to dissect a mouse, the female's sensitivity is undoubtedly enhanced by sensory bristles. Jens Wahlstedt thought that perhaps the bristles or "brush feathers" of the female played a role in stimulating a young owl to open its bill and snap at food.

Bill-snapping, in which the lower mandible is forcibly thrust against the upper, producing a click or snap, is commonly given by most species of owls in aggressive or defensive situations, functioning as a warning sound like the growl of a dog. Close observations of a captive Great Gray Owl revealed that the sound is produced when the lower bill or mandible is thrust forward beyond the bill tip, pressed against the tip and then slipped back off to snap against the upper bill. Even young nestling Great Gray Owls bill-snap when handled. In trying to bring females in range of our snare we usually prodded the young birds, eliciting bill-snapping until they were too tired to respond. In June

1979 I learned that imitating the sound, in this case tapping one stone against another, worked even better! A harsh, hissing sound is often given under similar circumstances. Bill-snapping and hissing occur in both young and adult Great Grays, appearing in nestlings at an early age.

A defensive, crouching attitude commonly observed in Long-eared Owls and some other species, in which the back feathers are raised, the partly spread and raised wings are held forward, and the tail is spread, while the bird snaps its bill and hisses, has only occasionally been observed in the Great Gray. Al Oeming, who photographed a female Great Gray in this posture, mentions that it did this when a Red-tailed Hawk was diving at it, and when a dog was present at the nest site. An immature female owl kept by me for two weeks in November 1977 showed this defensive behavior on several occasions. It displayed the posture while perched on the back of a couch, in response to the sudden appearance of our full-grown English springer spaniel. The appearance and approach of our cat elicited even stronger display. In addition to bill-snapping and hissing, the wings were spread and lowered, the head was brought down (and directed toward the dog or cat), and—most striking of all—the scapular feathers were fully erected. However, the wings, although partly spread, were not raised and brought forward as in the typical Long-eared Owl display. On approaching a tree with an active nest in Saskatchewan, the female being on the nest and the male on a limb nearby, Clifford Law noted: "When I was about twenty yards from the tree with the nest, the owl sitting on the limb lowered its wings, ruffled its feathers and started to snap its beak." Nothing like this was seen by us, the male being fairly shy in most cases. This points out the variability of behavior in the species. An apparently similar display was observed in Finland. Erkki Pulliainen and Kaleni Loisa reported that "The male Owl defended its

While the attentive female shelters her brood from the sun, a downy owlet begins gulping down a whole vole, which had been delivered to the nest by a male.

A few days after this photo was taken, the nest collapsed, probably as a result of the pushing and shoving of the young. The still flightless owlets dropped safely thirty-five feet to the forest floor. Within a few days, they were able to climb up into nearby trees. The male continued to deliver food to the young while the female remained near.

nest against an attacking Goshawk by spreading its wings and ruffling its plumage."

In the Great Gray Owl, normal roosting behavior provides fairly effective concealment. Perched close to the trunk of a mature aspen tree, a Great Gray blends so well as to be almost invisible. With head lowered, eyes closed, and facial discs "folded," the face is divided by a vertical dark line that matches streaks on the tree trunk. The streaked plumage of breast and belly are equally suitable camouflage patterns. There is another feature of Great Gray plumage that may also function in concealment. It is a trait found in many other species of owls. Owing to a diffuse pattern on the sides of the head, neck, and especially the upper breast, these areas seem out of our focus, whether viewed in life or in a photograph. The effect is partly the result of light penetrating semitransparent feathers. In the Great Gray there is a charcoal-gray and black pattern; never quite distinct, the shadowy, grayish tones blend smoothly together.

Most owls have a patch of light-colored or whitish feathers at the base of the chin. Usually these feathers are exposed prominently during the upright concealment posture; this disruptive color pattern effectively interrupts the darker form of the vertical body. In the Great Gray Owl the white patch, which is separated into two bars by blackish feathers in the middle of the foreneck, is almost always fully exposed. Law thought that at a distance the feathers looked like a "white moustache." These feathers are glossy white in both sexes. Because they reflect so much light, on a dark day or late in the evening they often may be a means for identifying the species. This distinctive feature of Great Gray Owl plumage may also function as a species recognition signal. Some observers have reported that the white patches are larger in females than in males. Others have noted individual differences in this character; the supposed differences may

A sleeping owl perched close to the trunk of an aspen poplar practically disappears from view.

partly be related to the bird's behavior and the extent to which the white patches are exposed.

The delicate pattern and subtle colors of its plumage can best be appreciated by looking at Robert Taylor's photographs, taken of several individuals under a variety of light conditions. An additional feature is the occurrence of a white margin on the outer scapulars or shoulder feathers, a trait shared with several species of owls. In some individuals this white mark is pronounced, appearing as a definite stripe at the base of each wing.

Great Gray Owls, like other birds, groom or preen, stretching in all directions as agilely as contortionists to reach nearly all parts of their plumage with bill or foot. By running feathers through the bill, dirt is removed and the complex interlocking structure of each feather is maintained. To reach its throat feathers an owl bends its head sharply forward, then, wagging its head from side to side, works its bill down the length of each feather. In methodical fashion it straightens and arranges feathers of the breast, back, and wings, occasionally reaching around to the rump, raising the feathers that overlap the base of the tail and vigorously rubbing its bill into this area. An oil-secreting gland at the upper base of the tail provides a dressing for the plumage. When the gland is pressed an oily substance oozes out and is transferred to the bill and thence, in the course of preening, to the feathers. It is a vital process. When the thin, oily film on feathers is exposed to sunlight, some of it is changed to vitamin D. Through subsequent preening a small amount of this altered oil is ingested, thus providing birds with a substitute source of this needed vitamin. Owls have relatively large oil glands, even compared to waterfowl. Owls need to sun themselves and so we may sometimes find them on the edge of woods, perched with closed eyes, facing toward the bright sun.

On one occasion only, I saw a Great Gray Owl "sun-bathing." This curious reaction, whereby an individual rigidly holds its head or body at an angle to sunlight, has been reported for a wide range of birds. The bird I saw was a female brooding young on June 2, 1970, in a high, exposed nest in northern Minnesota. For almost a minute, while I watched from less than twelve feet away and at the level of the nest, she held her head sideways to the sun, with her bill open and her eyes closed.

An owl preens its face with its talons, lifting one foot to clean all about its head and bill. Sometimes the feathers of the ear region are attacked as vigorously and audibly as when a cat scratches behind its ear. Undoubtedly, feather lice and other parasites occasionally provoke a bout of irritated scratching, just as fleas annoy dogs and cats. Extended preening of the whole body often follows head scratching. After preening, a Great Gray, like most birds, gives a comfort-shake to adjust its plumage, shaking itself heavily, then ruffling its head feathers.

Development of especially long talons has not eliminated the necessary manual dexterity that owls require to carry out a variety of tasks, notwithstanding that the bill is used for this purpose in many ways. Watching a Great Gray Owl in our family room feeding itself, I was surprised to see how it handled small food items. With talons closed, the owl used its knuckles, that is, the joints at the base of the talons of the two anterior toes, to pick up and hold small pieces of meat, raising the foot to transfer food to its bill.

Feathers of all owls are relatively soft-edged, reducing the sound of their movements. Because of this, when hovering over prey they may be able to hear better and are less likely to be heard. Great Grays, specialists in the pursuit of small mammals, have feathers that are unusually soft and their flight must be nearly noiseless.

A tail feather from a Great Gray Owl provides a lesson in beauty and adaptability. Twelve inches long and two and one-half inches wide, it is a reminder of the large tail of this relatively small-bodied bird. The feather's light weight is impressive; despite its size, it floats to the floor when dropped, and it lifts with the slightest breath. Considering the function of the tail, an individual feather is remarkably soft and flexible. Mottled grayish brown, with alternating light and dark bars, it appears denser than it is. When pressed against a printed page the letters show through clearly, even through the darkest parts, and the grayish-white bars and spots seem almost nonexistent. The central two tail feathers, which are longer and usually grayer (or brown, if faded) than the others, are nearly transparent, colored objects being visible through the vanes even when held eight inches away.

Great Gray Owl body feathers also are exceptionally long, a feature noted by Ernest S. Norman, a Manitoba farmer, who reported: "One morning in February, 1918, I noticed an unusually long and fluffy feather hanging in a willow bush near my barn. I at once knew that it was that of an owl, but had never met here any species of owls with such tremendously long feathers. Several days later the puzzle was solved, when, in broad daylight a Great Gray Owl (the first one and only one that I have seen) flew to a shade tree in front of our house. It stayed around for several weeks after that."

Great Gray breast feathers may be more than nine inches long. They are highly filamentous for most of their length, bearing long, downy plumes except for the distal inch or two. Though the filaments or plumes arise laterally from the feather shaft, as do the vanes, they are extremely light and airy, floating off in all directions as if repelled electrically, giving the feather a cylindrical form. They move freely, responding instantly to the least movement of air, trembling and swinging

about like the feathery appendages of some sea animal. Thus, even the contour feathers provide a remarkable degree of insulation. It is this downy aspect as much as the distinctive color and pattern that makes it possible to readily identify feathers from a Great Gray Owl.

In spite of their heavily feathered appearance, Great Gray Owls, as do most birds, have areas of the body surface that are featherless. These apteria, as they are called, include an almost inch-wide strip down the sternum to the vent, noticeable only after considerable parting of the abundant, downy bases of adjacent feathers. Even larger, though concealed by overlapping feathers, is an area under each wing, running from the neck and shoulder, across the side of the breast and onto the thigh. The under-wing apteria provide a significant means of losing heat. Overheated birds droop their wings, exposing their armpits, so to speak, thus helping to lower their body temperature through a cooling effect on blood vessels. On a warm day, adults handled for banding frequently do this after being released. It also is a sign of stress and distress, and a warning; a female, upset over disturbance of her young, may droop her wings prior to attacking. Heat reduction is also obtained through panting, a behavior often seen in nestlings as well as grown birds.

One day in mid-April 1979 we banded and released an owl in a large, open area with a few tamarack trees and some willows near the road. It was a dull, misty day and the ground was still covered with deep, wet snow. Upon release, the bird flew a short distance away, fluorescent-green tail gleaming, and landed on the snow. After standing for a few minutes, ruffling its feathers and staring back at us, it began walking across the snow, deliberately placing one foot before the other, moving with a heavy, waddling gait, not using its wings at all. Immediately I thought of the name given this bird by Indians along the Yukon River in Alaska;

according to zoologist William H. Dall (reported by Bent), the owl was called *nūhl-tūhl,* meaning "heavy walker." After a few minutes, posed motionless on the broad snowfield, the owl flew a short distance to another slightly elevated prominence, folded its wings, and again slowly walked about as if searching for something. When the owl repeated the sequence a third time, I was convinced the name was appropriate. If Indians saw Great Gray Owls walking on top of snow in this fashion, then I could understand their use of the name "heavy walker."

This incident also reminded me of an observation made of a wintering Great Gray Owl near Ottawa in 1969. Dan Brunton had followed a bird into a cedar thicket where it had gone, evidently searching for mice. His field notes record: "As I approached, the bird literally ran out from under the trees into the open . . . its tracks showed it definitely was running, one foot in front of the other. . . ."

Although its feet are small in proportion to its body size, one must remember that this is a relatively light-bodied bird. The feathers on the toes are lighter than in the Snowy Owl, but except for bare soles and three yellow scutes at the upper base of each talon, the feet are covered with short, dense, furlike feathers, undoubtedly an aid in walking or running on top of snow.

The owl kept in my home for a short period in November 1977 was so gentle I was able to let it perch on my bare fist; the bird rarely showed any inclination to tighten its talons. Thus I discovered that the soles of the feet were warm, a slight but oddly satisfying observation.

Like the Barred Owl, its close relative, the Great Gray Owl may be said to emit a hooting sound, but this statement fails to convey any semblance of the vocal capability of the species. It is doubtful whether written descriptions can properly portray the quality and variety of its vocalizations. A low, mellow hooting announces the presence of the male, a series of regularly spaced notes of equal duration and interval and up to eight or twelve in succession, being the primary territorial song. Toward the end of a sequence the notes are given more rapidly and with decreasing volume. Reporting on a detailed study in Sweden, Wahlstedt describes this call, which he notes as being fairly weak compared to other species of owls, as a series of pumping sounds given about one and a half times per second. He observed that in certain body positions the tail wagged inward at each note. The call is reported to be audible under ideal conditions up to eight hundred meters. The male's territorial call may be given not only in early spring but also late in the breeding season in June and July.

Another call, used by both sexes and heard less often, consists of a series of double notes, given more rapidly (about three times per second according to Wahlstedt), and up to as many as a hundred times in one sequence. It is evidently a defensive or warning cry. It is weaker than the male's territorial call, carrying only about fifty meters, but it is given with great vigor.

A variety of rasping, screeching, cooing, or whistling calls have been described by several authors for both male and female Great Gray Owls. Probably most common is a soft mellow hoot or *Whoop!,* often given by the female on the nest as a means of communicating with the male. Hungry chicks give rapid, chattering, or chirping notes, a pleasant sound; when older they give harsh, rasping *Sher-rick!* calls. Wanting food for herself or, more likely, for her hungry young, the female calls softly or loudly: *"Sher-rick!,"* or gives an extended *"Shreek!"* Well-grown nestlings or birds that have left the nest may give the *Sher-rick!* begging call repeatedly. My observations agree with those of Valdemar Berggren and Jens Wahlstedt; reporting on a detailed study of vocalizations in the Great Gray Owl, they stated: "The female's call when fed by the male and during copulation is shown to be a reminiscence of the begging calls of the chicks and juveniles, and advertises the female's willingness to be approached by the male." This is the case in many bird species.

Somewhat similar vocalizations were given by the closely related Barred Owl during an apparent distraction display by a female with fledglings nearby, according to an observation described by David M. Bird and Jo Wright. Parmelee describes similar behavior for the Snowy Owl out on open tundra.

During alarm situations, the female often utters a loud, drawn-out sound that appears to be an extreme form of the begging call. And the strangest calls of this species are undoubtedly those given by the female during injury-feigning or distraction display. The greater the distress, the more extreme the calls. A loud, heronlike squawk or bark climaxes a series of notes ranging from vigorous hooting to high-pitched wails and squeals, all expressing great anxiety. This is probably the basis for many unusual calls ascribed in the literature to this species. (For a description of extreme distraction display, see pp. 130-31).

Vocalizations carry meaning not only in terms of specific syllables, but in intonation and strength as well. Thus, the numerous calls given by Great Gray Owls can, and do, vary according to different situations. In short, a wider range of vocal communication occurs in Great Gray Owls than is indicated here.

7

Short Days and Long Nights

It is twenty degrees below zero on a sunny day in January. Two feet of snow cover the ground. Near a spruce bog, a Great Gray Owl hunches on an aspen stub at the edge of an opening in the woods. Except for quick movements of its head, the owl is motionless, its mottled gray and white plumage blending with the pale and scarred bark of the tree.

Beneath the snow, fifty feet away, a little red-backed vole ascends a ventilation shaft, a frozen, crystalline tunnel leading to a small hole on the surface. Restless, it ventures from the warmer, burrow-ridden, leafy ground level to the icy, cold air above. The vole is surely dazzled by its first glimpse of the daytime world.

For the Great Gray Owl, patiently following each minute sound with gleaming eyes, the appearance of the vole has a galvanic effect. The owl launches forward with its powerful feet, wings unfolding with the precision of an umbrella mechanism, into a fast, steady glide that ends with a sudden downward pounce. One long, clawed foot arrives first, grabbing the vole securely; a swirl of snow particles shimmers momentarily in the bright light, then settles about the bulky, feathered creature.

For a moment the owl is motionless again, staring vacantly as it crouches with broad wings and tail outspread, flight feathers splayed upon the immaculate surface of the snow. Its ivory-smooth bill and bright, yellow eyes are like jewels set in dead wood. Sparkling snow crystals lie on the stricken vole's reddish-brown fur; locked in the owl's talons it is already dead, and a bright drop of blood, a crimson bead, lies in the snow beside it. Then the owl bends down, nips the vole sharply with its bill, brings its head up and swallows the warm, furry body with three gulps, saliva glistening along the hard edge of its bill.

Winter is a critical period for many animals. For Great Gray Owls, depending chiefly on small mammals—mice, voles, shrews—for food, availability of this restricted prey must be a significant factor in their distribution and movements. In Finland, according to Heimo Mikkola, these birds eat about four or fewer mice daily during summer months. Low temperatures of winter make greater demands on all organisms, however, and Great Grays probably eat far more in such periods. This is supported by W. Earl Godfrey's observation in the Ottawa district of one capturing and devouring five mice in half an hour. Probably, owls eat as much as they can catch, storing up fat against days when they are unable to get food. In exceptionally cold weather, time and effort spent searching for prey must be measured against the return. Staying close to good hunting grounds and resting for long periods, insulated by their heavy plumage, means saving energy, and reduces the amount of food needed to survive.

Faced with a scarcity of prey species, they can search for new hunting grounds, flying into new and unfamiliar country, settling down for long periods where mice are available, or making long, unsuccessful flights into areas where there are no mice. In the Scandinavian countries, on numerous occasions large numbers have perished from lack of food. Unable to find sufficient prey, faced with dwindling body reserves, they may become lethargic, appearing tamer than usual. Thomas Nuttall, the gifted English botanist and ornithologist, reported that Great Grays were ". . . occasionally seen in Massachusetts in the depth of severe winters. One was caught perched on a wood-pile, in a state of listless inactivity, in the morning after daylight, at Marblehead, in February, 1831. This individual survived for several months, and showed a great partiality for fish and birds." That owl, it may be noted, attracted the attention of John James Audubon. The great bird artist and

naturalist hurried to the scene, undoubtedly anxious to see his first live Great Gray Owl. One can still sense his disappointment upon finding when he arrived, as he noted later, that "it had died, and I could not trace its remains." Maurice Street, a meticulous birder, describes how a farmer in central Saskatchewan caught a weak and thin bird by hand in December 1955. Fed raw meat, "it became so tame it would follow him about the yard, even into his house. Unfortunately, it lived little more than a week."

Accounts of Great Grays feeding on carrion are few. In March 1974 a bird was reported eating fat and remnants of flesh from the remains of a butchered moose carcass in a yard close to a house in southeastern Manitoba. The bird seemed unafraid of people and paid little attention to two adult Saint Bernard dogs. This observation of carrion feeding is difficult to understand since there was an abundance of voles in the immediate vicinity; however, the snow was very deep at the time. For the same winter there is a report of apparent predation and cannibalism by an adult Great Gray Owl in Alberta. Bob Fisher observed one owl perched atop a still warm carcass of another that was slightly eaten. It was believed that the owl had attacked a weak or dying bird. Some Great Grays observed feeding on snowshoe hares and other large prey may have been feeding on road-kills. I have several reports of owls seen feeding on snowshoe hares caught in snares. It is not clear, however, whether in any of these cases the owl killed a struggling hare or was feeding on an already dead animal. In one observation, when approached by the trapper, the owl attempted unsuccessfully to fly away with the carcass, and was reluctant to leave. Robert Stitt wrote from Moosonee, Ontario, that he had found a hare completely removed from a snare. All that remained was a bit of hair and blood. Previously, martens had occasionally eaten snared hares, but he thought it unlikely a marten could consume an entire hare at one feeding. In addition to fresh marten tracks, he found a large feather from a Great Gray Owl at the site. At another time, Stitt, upon returning to his camp, saw a Great Gray Owl fly up from a spot near a pile of marten carcasses partly buried in the snow. At first the owl perched on a nearby ten-gallon gas drum, then flew away. One or two marten carcasses had been moved a foot or so away from the others, and there were wing marks in the snow. My informant presumed the owl had just begun scavenging. Ability to feed on carrion could help carry an owl through a period of food scarcity.

Although Great Gray Owls feed almost exclusively on small mammals, other prey occasionally are taken, for example, red squirrel, Norway rat, pocket gophers, moles, and weasels; duck, grouse, and songbirds. Still, I was surprised to find remains of an adult Sharp-tailed Grouse in a nest in June 1979. That's a heavy load, and I wonder how the male carried it to the nest, if indeed he brought the entire grouse. At the other extreme, a United States customs officer described to me how one night a Great Gray Owl pounced on a dragonfly fluttering about on the roadway beneath a bright light!

Despite the evidence that Great Gray Owls can capture small birds, the report of one collected many years ago with thirteen redpolls in its stomach is puzzling. I can't imagine a Great Gray catching that many active, sparrow-sized birds in one day. This particular specimen, a female, was obtained by Dall on April 11, 1868, near Nulato, Alaska, as noted by Bent. Perhaps the owl found a night roost or a flock of exhausted birds floundering in the snow after a severe coldsnap or snowstorm.

Recent published reports of Great Gray Owls being a threat to poultry strike me as an exaggeration of their known behavior. Thomas S. Roberts writes about a Great Gray Owl that killed two fowl by entering a henhouse one December, but this appears to be a solitary and singular episode. I have several times assured local farmers or landowners that the large owl perched near their buildings was hunting mice, not house cats or domestic rabbits! On several occasions we captured a Great Gray Owl near a farm home, taking the bird indoors to demonstrate its docile nature and other characteristics. Even strong skeptics have changed their opinion of this bird after seeing one being measured at the kitchen table.

Attracting the attention of all observers who have watched these owls closely in winter, whether on their northern breeding grounds or elsewhere, is their ability to locate prey by sound alone. This capacity is most apparent in winter when owls are successfully capturing mice from deep beneath the snow, though it is of obvious advantage in hunting in heavy vegetation, in low light, and at night.

As often as not, when they turn those big heads they are simply directing their ears toward some intriguing sound, some faint scuttling in the grass. So their eyes sweep past us, seeming vague and unfixed as they concentrate on sound. Lacking their ability to probe beneath the snow, we are often puzzled by their actions. Late one winter evening we found a bird perched about ten feet high in a tree, engrossed in an event near the base. The owl stared down intently toward the blank surface of the snow, ignoring me as I carried in a live-trap to first a hundred, then fifty, and finally twenty-five feet. All the while, it paid scant attention to me, but kept peering steadily downward. After several minutes, during which the mouse in the trap, numb with cold and barely active, drew no response from the owl, I retrieved the trap. With some haste because of the growing darkness, Bob Taylor set out to try to capture the owl using a wire snare on the end of a long pole. To our surprise, he went right up to the bird and from directly in front of it began the difficult task of trying to fit the wire loop over its head. At that height and in the poor light, Taylor was unable to see the snare. An agonizing effort to bring the invisible snare into position followed; twice the pole bumped the owl's breast, but, absurdly, the owl paid no attention! When Taylor made a final, desperate attempt, the end of the pole hit the bird's bill. With a startled look, the owl shook itself, looked at his would-be captor as if suddenly seeing him for the first time, then unfolded his wings and flew off into the night.

When attempting to lure owls from distant perches we usually relied on a squeaking sound. With this we could get their attention, even from distances of a hundred yards or more. Law noted: "As the Great Gray Owl sits, slowly turning its head from side to side and sometimes looking straight down below it, we learn to know that it is picking up the sound of a mouse chewing up straw or grain. Silently it sails off its perch to a distance of about sixty yards, hovers over a spot for a few minutes and then drops suddenly down into the soft snow. After remaining motionless for a couple of minutes, it slowly raises one foot out of the snow with a dead mouse in its talons. The owl then proceeds to swallow the mouse whole, and after that it flies back to its perch or to another tree limb nearby"

Recent studies of hearing ability in Barn Owls have shown that this species can readily locate and capture prey in the total absence of light, relying on sound perception alone. Further, it has been discovered that they respond to a fairly specific range and type of sound, especially faint, rustling noises. So it should be no surprise that Great Grays can hear and locate mice beneath snow.

As reported by Law and others, the characteristic manner in which Great Grays capture prey beneath snow is by dropping down from a perch or from an almost motionless hovering position.

While hovering, the birds can look down almost between their feet. From this position they can get a good auditory fix on their prey. Usually, they then drop in a quick pounce, their long legs reaching down in readiness to seize prey. Godfrey noted that they did this with "legs extended fully, the thrust of the talons reaching to the ground under eight inches of snow." Brunton and Pittaway reported that a bird would hover "with legs dangling" and would then "crash into the snow and capture prey." As early as 1772 similar behavior was observed at Severn, Ontario, by Andrew Graham, who stated (and his observation was published almost verbatim by Nuttall fifty years later): "It chiefly resorts to the woods and fly [sic] in pairs living on mice, hares, etc. It flies very low yet seizes its prey with such force that in winter it will make a hole in the snow about a foot deep."

Our previous observations, and the above published descriptions of owls capturing prey in winter, gave little hint of the extraordinary behavior we were to see in owls hunting under deep snow conditions, especially in late winter 1973–74 and thereafter. Again and again, while we looked on with wonder, owls plunged deep into the snow in pursuit of prey, often briefly disappearing altogether. Typically, an owl would fly out from a perch, hover over the snow—apparently taking a final bearing on its prey—then partly fold its wings and plummet downward into the snow, sometimes vertically, at times at an angle. They did this so often and so successfully it would appear that this is an adaptation for preying upon small mammals in the deep, soft snow characteristic of northern forests.

The spectacle of these solemn-faced, relatively clumsy-looking owls sailing forth on their huge wings, then suddenly folding up and diving face downward into snowbanks astounded us. Much in the manner of terns, ospreys, and other birds that dive into water for prey, Great Gray

In this sequence, photographed at four frames per second, an owl fixes the location of prey under snow by sound, hovers, turns about, and plunges into the snow. It missed! Some idea of the speed of the dive may be gained from noting the position of the bird relative to the tree on the right in the last four photos.

Owls flung themselves into snow with the same carefree appearance. Observation and study of films and photographs revealed that though at times the feet were brought forward under the chin at the last moment, the plunge was often made with the feet well back under the tail, the owl entering the snow face foremost. The wings were closed at the last moment, but held out from the body so that they provided a brake, preventing the bird from going in too deep. Nevertheless, owls repeatedly plunged right out of sight, and occasionally remained below the surface for half a minute or more. Still, their wings, though not always visible to an observer, were usually on or close to the surface of the snow. Sometimes they emerged from the snow by raising themselves up on their spread primaries. Thus, the wings served not only to help absorb the shock of the plunge, but also to permit the bird to return to the surface.

Since Great Gray Owls have long legs, we wondered at first why they should have to exert themselves in this strenuous fashion. We finally decided that they were crashing down through soft snow to try for mice otherwise out of reach. The sudden and unexpected collapse of snow caused by an owl's plunge apparently demolished tunnels leaving a mouse or vole confused and cut off from escape. Once having plunged into snow after prey targeted by sound, the owls attempted to capture them with their feet. Often, when the back of an owl was above the snow we could see that it was making grappling motions, and foot and claw marks in the bottom of fresh holes gave a clear picture of this behavior. Their long talons permit an especially wide grasp, toes and talons spreading close to four inches fore and aft, doubtless a great assistance in making this kind of blind capture. By making a plunge and thrusting down with their feet, they could reach prey as deep as eighteen inches.

Owls that we saw capture prey often rested briefly, half-buried in the snow, then put their heads down to their feet, brought up a mouse with their bill and swallowed it with a few quick gulps. Dan Brunton noticed that they usually made a quick scan of the field around them for danger before proceeding to eat. After feeding, they frequently remained in the same place, at times with wings outspread, before returning to a perch. The appearance of an owl in this situation is aptly described by Earl Godfrey: "Once, in deep soft snow, the wings and bulky feathers were spread out over a surprising area, looking at a distance like a rug with an owl's head on it!" Brunton suggested that the spread wings could serve the owl as a glare guard, a means of reducing light reflected from the snow, and he thought it was done less often on cloudy days. Perhaps the dark gray or blackish feathers adjacent to the inner edge of their eyes serve the same function. In soft snow the outspread wings and tail also keep the bird on the surface, enabling it to rest. We couldn't always tell, when watching owls in action, if those that plunged out of sight were successful, but it seemed that a bird that missed prey flew up shortly afterward. Examination of some holes revealed a drop or two of blood, which we assumed to be evidence of a kill. On the other hand, on a few occasions when we saw an owl swallow prey, we were unable to find any blood in the hole.

Depth of plunge-holes varied, apparently depending on the total depth and softness of the snow, as well as the level at which the prey species were active. Where the major vegetative cover beneath the snow was alfala and, especially, sweet clover, meadow voles frequently fed at some distance above ground, judging by droppings and other evidence that we found in plunge-holes. The force with which owls plunged into snow could be appreciated by the degree of compaction of snow in the bottom of a hole. Inverted cone-shaped masses of crystallized snow almost a foot

An owl has come and gone, leaving a distinct and lovely plunge-mark in the snow.

layer of snow on top of the crust preserved good impressions. At one hole, the wing length could easily be measured, and at five other holes an impression of an owl's face was visible, including in one case even the outline of the bill! These birds were apparently unable to break through the crust with their heads, or weren't trying, but in each instance they had been able to break through with their feet. The manner in which they plopped their faces against the crust made us wonder if the heavy facial disc feathers might not also provide protection for snow plunging.

Once we saw an owl, hunting along a line of utility poles a half-mile from any trees, plunge face-downward onto hard-packed drift snow beside a road. When the owl struck the snow it crumpled up and was still; I was sure it had broken its neck, for the bird had made no impression on the hard surface. A moment later, however, it raised its head, stood looking about for a second or two, then flew back up onto the pole.

Sometimes a successful bird would sit in the snow for a minute or more after swallowing its prey, and one bird had its head out of sight for a measured forty-five seconds. In late winter and spring, when occasionally the snow was wet and heavy, a plunging owl would have some difficulty getting back up onto the surface. We often wished we were close enough to net them, for at times it appeared that they were stuck in the snow.

I didn't really notice until March 14, 1979, that when an owl made a vertical plunge, the wings were partly withdrawn at the last moment so that for the final five feet there was a rapid acceleration. I noted this under perfect lighting conditions and later determined that this was the usual case. Also, at times plunging birds went so deep even the wrists went into the snow, so that only the tips of the primaries and tips of the tail feathers stuck up above the surface.

thick were removed from some old holes.

We often discussed what the owls would do if and when a crust formed on the snow. After this happened, they continued, to our surprise, to dive into the snow, breaking through quarter-inch and half-inch crusts. In mid-March 1974, when there was a one-inch crust under two inches of fresh snow, we checked a number of fresh holes in a field favored by three Great Gray Owls. The snow depth over the field ranged from twenty-three to thirty inches. Plunge-holes in several cases were made by birds mainly using their feet. These holes went down as much as ten inches, giving an idea of the reach of their legs. But some birds, judging by the evidence, had plunged head downward, even through this crust, whole bodies going down six or ten inches. The thin

It is curious that we did not observe snow-plunging until February 7, 1974. We had watched Great Gray Owls hunting in winter on many days in previous years, but this behavior was not noticed then; thereafter, it was seen each winter when we found owls.

Whether shallow or deep, plunge-holes left by Great Grays almost always have distinctive, crescent-shaped marks left by the folded wings on initial impact, as well as a fainter pattern of the spread primaries where the bird braced itself to lift out of the hole. Often, an impression of the tail can also be seen. Where owls were regularly pursuing prey in this way, plunge-holes were abundant. Thereafter, we frequently identified Great Gray Owl feeding sites by these characteristic signs of their

A burrow opening in the snow. Mice, voles, and shrews burrow to the surface after a fresh snowfall.

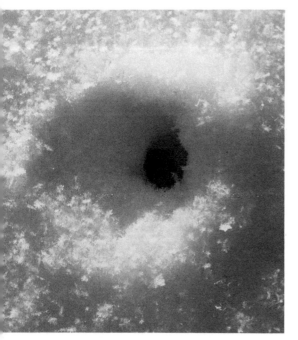

presence, looking at roadside snowbanks while driving through owl country. Plunge-holes often can be identified after they are many days old and even after a light snowfall. We have since found these distinctive signs almost everywhere we have seen owls.

Nothing in our previous experience, however, had quite prepared us for the sight of 128 fresh plunge-holes along a mile stretch on one side of a road. It was a bright day in late January, five days after a snowfall, and the numerous impressions were conspicuous on the otherwise smooth, white surface.

Herb Copland and I once saw a Hawk Owl plunge into soft snow, apparently hunting prey by sound. Since Hawk Owl-sized plunge-marks are rare, even where these birds are frequently seen, this is presumably an uncommon hunting technique in this species. Ornithologist Richard Knapton told me he watched a hunting Boreal Owl repeatedly plunge into snow in a wooded area near Winnipeg. Both species have the capacity to do this, but evidently employ it less often than does the Great Gray Owl.

The small eyes of Great Gray Owls, relative to their body size, as mentioned earlier, appear to be linked to daytime hunting, presumably another trait associated with long daylength in far northern latitudes. Great Grays can see surprisingly well, even in bright sunlight over snow, and it appears that their visual acuity serves them well. In early February at midday we watched a Great Gray fly out

No two plunge-holes are exactly alike, as the pictures on these two pages show. In some cases, an owl may jump about in the same hole in an effort to catch a mouse, making puzzling impressions.

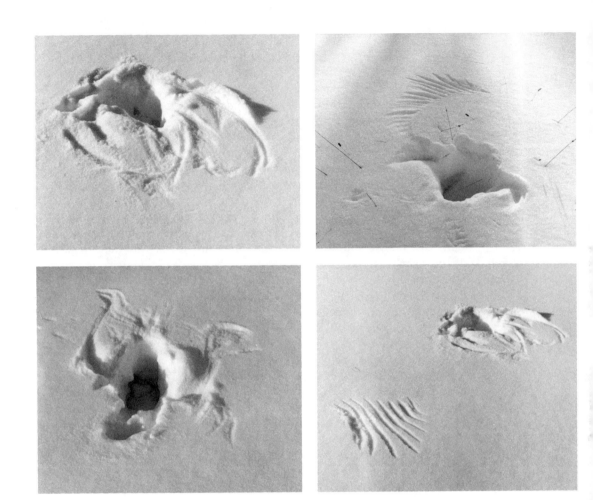

with rapid wingbeats over an open field for at least two hundred yards to pounce on what we presumed was a vole on top of the snow. Similarly, Brunton and Pittaway reported seeing a Great Gray Owl in February fly approximately two hundred yards to snatch up a small mammal on the snow, apparently having seen the prey from that distance.

Nevertheless, Great Gray Owls are usu-

ally most active during periods of low light in early morning and late afternoon and evening. Dull, overcast skies and falling snow produce similar conditions, sometimes bringing birds out in numbers. Although strong winds tend to keep them in the woods, occasionally we have found a Great Gray Owl on an exposed perch, feathers ruffling in the wind like loose clothing, staring across open fields.

8

Feathers on the Snow

Reaching far out on swaying birch branches, a Ruffed Grouse snips off six more buds, each time with an audible snap, then, bobbing its head as it seeks to regain its balance, it stands upright, poised against the gray, late evening, winter sky. Throat bulging with brown, resinous buds, the grouse ruffles its plumage, then flies off, wings clattering against twigs. Making a fast glide into a nearby tamarack grove, it changes perches twice, then, as is its nightly habit in winter, quietly dives into a snowbank in an open space between two trees.

In early morning light a Great Gray Owl, hungry after a cold night spent motionless on its perch, blinks its eyes, shifts from one foot to the other, then shakes out its feathers. The gray hunter drops down and drifts on broad wings through the frosty air, then rises abruptly, settling lightly onto a favorite perch on the tip of a dead tamarack, watchful, listening, head turning from one point to another. The first chickadee calls, plaintive awakening notes, then the owl suddenly cocks its head downward, its whole attention brought to a focus on the blank surface of the snow. Snug in its overnight cave, the grouse stirs, nibbles at the snow, then pushes upwards, thrusting its head out into the daylight. Sighting the small, dark object, the owl at once pounces, seizing the grouse's head, but the unexpected thrashing of wings brings it off balance. Leaning back on its tail the owl struggles to right itself, then bends forward, crushing the back of the feathered head with its bill. For a few seconds longer the grouse's wings futilely pound the snow.

Intent on plucking its prey, the owl fails to hear the soft footfalls of a rapidly approaching lynx. Padding lightly across the snow, the cat springs while the owl's head is down. One quick bite amid a flurry of wings, and the lynx has made its kill. Ears laid back, it pulls and tears at the owl carcass, feathers drifting across the snow. It devours all of the owl's scanty flesh, shearing off the long flight feathers as, with head tilted, it chews the wings. Rubbing one great, furry paw over its face to rid itself of clinging feathers, the lynx then sniffs at the half-buried grouse. In one quick motion it seizes the grouse in its jaws, turns, and pads quietly away.

Few accounts are available regarding natural enemies of the Great Gray Owl. Oeming suggested that black bears climb to nests to prey on young raptors, but without referring to a specific example of predation on the Great Gray Owl. We saw what appeared to be old claw marks on limbs near an occupied nest, fifty feet above ground. The Great Horned Owl appears to be a fairly serious cause of mortality. Oeming described a case in Alberta where one apparently killed and ate a Great Gray Owl, and three similar cases were reported to him by a trapper. One was observed near Lac du Bonnet, Manitoba, January 10, 1978, feeding upon a Great Gray Owl on the ice next to a small island. When approached, the owl made threatening signs and attempted to fly off with its prey, but it was left alone. The next day it was discovered that the victim was an adult female banded by us a month earlier about eight miles southward. In March 1978 remains of a second Great Gray Owl were found about six miles away on top of fresh snow in a situation suggesting predation by another Great Horned Owl. On May 5, 1979, in the same region, old Great Gray Owl feathers were found beneath a man-made nest; I estimated they were from a young owl possibly killed in July 1978. Mallard feathers were found at the same site. Presumably the nest where the feathers were found had served as a feeding platform for a Great Horned Owl that had raised three young in a nest about three hundred yards away. At least two other man-made nests were used as feeding platforms by Great Horned Owls. When biologists John and Frank Craighead released a captive Great Gray Owl within the nesting territory of a pair of Great Horned Owls, however, it established a temporary range and was not molested by the resident birds. When snowshoe hare populations are high and nest sites are limited, the Great Horned Owl may be a strong competitor as well as a predator.

In the previous chapter I mentioned a possible case of predation by a Great Gray Owl. According to Alex Lawrence, a Manitoba taxidermist found the remains of a Great Gray in the stomach of a Golden Eagle. The same species was reported by Nils Höglund and Erik Lansgren as a possible predator on the Great Gray in Sweden. A Goshawk attacked and killed a Great Gray Owl in Finland in the summer of 1978; this unusual incident was observed by Antti Leinonen and reported to me by Mikkola. An adult Great Gray Owl found dead on a roadside near Lac du Bonnet, Manitoba, on April 11, 1979, may have been the victim of an attack by Common Crows. When I received the bird I assumed it had been struck by a vehicle, but upon preparing it as a study skin I found only a shallow puncture wound in the outer edge of one eye, just deep enough to penetrate the brain. The small hole in the skull was wedge-shaped and could have been made by a crow's bill. Common Crows were reported active in the vicinity. A month earlier, two local residents of the same area told us that one of two Great Gray Owls seen near their home had been harassed by crows early in the morning. This was the first day that spring we saw crows, and they were fairly abundant. In the previous winter, birder Ray Tuokko saw a flock of crows harass and drive a Great Gray Owl into the cover of dense spruce trees. Common Ravens, on the other hand, which are frequently seen in the vicinity of Great Grays in winter, have never shown any aggression toward them or hardly any interest in them.

Even on its breeding grounds the Great Gray Owl has probably always been subject to some mortality by man. As reported by ornithologist W. E. Clyde Todd in the early 1900s, this species was often killed by natives at Moose Factory on the James Bay coast: "Together with other owls, they are caught in pole-traps, set up in a conspicuous position, and all are used for food." Undoubtedly, the steel trap was used to take owls as soon as the early fur traders brought it into this country. Even today, Cree Indians living at Winisk on the Hudson Bay coastline of Ontario, about a hundred miles east of Severn, are reported to kill Great Gray Owls for food at every opportunity. Old Crow Indians of Alaska considered Great Gray Owls "not bad eating, while the slightly more common Great Horned Owls are not particularly good," Laurence Irving mentioned in a 1960 bulletin of the United States National Museum. Owls were seldom eaten, however, except when food was short. As recently as 1976, natives were given an open season on Snowy Owls in three wildlife management areas in Alaska.

Great Gray Owls have also been used by native people for other purposes. The skinned facial discs of Great Gray Owls seem to have had special significance. The stiff, flattened circlet of feathers was removed intact, together with the supporting skin, then the center portion was carefully decorated with beadwork, perhaps in imitation of an owl's eye, but sometimes with floral designs. Often only one disc, that is, the feathers surrounding one eye, was used, but occasionally both discs were sewn together. In 1969 I purchased two modern versions of these artifacts in a native handicraft shop at Churchill. One of them bore a beaded replica of the 1967 Canada Centennial design, an interesting example of acculturation. Both curios, it turned out, were made from owls shot by a Cree Indian in the winter of 1968–69 at Herchmer, ninety-five miles south of Churchill. There are reports that in earlier times Cree Indians attached these decorated discs to dwellings. They also were used as a decoration at the point of attachment of carrying strap "tump lines" for cradle boards.

Winnipeg wildlife photographer George Cotter told me he had observed a skin of a Great Gray nailed to the door of a Cree Indian house at Winisk, Ontario, in late winter, 1974, but no explanation was offered for the practice. And at Grand Rapids, Manitoba, in 1975, I was informed, a Cree Indian father hung a dead owl, apparently a Great Gray, on the door of his home as a kind of babysitter; so long as the owl was on the door his young daughter was afraid to go outside. This use of owls, and especially the preparation of owl facial discs, may be a cultural trait of some antiquity. The Ojibwa Indians of Parry Sound in Ontario, as reported by anthropologist Diamond Jenness in 1935, kept children indoors in the evening with an owl mask made from birch bark and hung outside the wigwam.

Once when Clyde Todd was in James Bay, the late Sam Waller, naturalist and museologist, gave him a Great Gray Owl facial disc skinned by Indians and obtained by him when he was teaching at Moose Factory from 1923 to 1930; Waller told me he thought that this was Todd's first record for the species in the region.

Great Grays also are accidentally taken, along with other owls, in traps set for furbearers. Mice and shrews scrambling about in search of bait on or near traps must lure many owls to death from starvation, exhaustion, or freezing. In the winter of 1926–27, of eighteen Great Grays brought to a taxidermist in northern Minnesota, almost all had been caught accidentally in steel traps set for weasels and other mammals. A trapper from that era told me that in some winters when mice and shrews were abundant and active, owls would eat the bait off his traps—worse, they would also eat his trapped weasels. Recently, biologists in Ontario found a dead Boreal Owl with its leg in a trap and a dead vole still clutched in its talons. A Manitoba trapper found a live Great Gray in a trap set for lynx, a dead Ruffed Grouse suspended above the trap serving as bait. Since one foot was frozen to the trap he severed it with an axe, thus freeing the bird. It flew up and

This Cree Indian artifact from Churchill, Manitoba, was made from a Great Gray Owl's facial disc feathers, the center portion decorated with beadwork on leather in imitation of an owl's eye.

Two sides of an owl's circlet of feathers were used in making this disc, which bears a replica in beads of the 1967 Canada Centennial design.

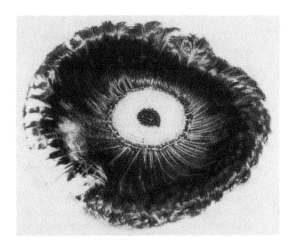

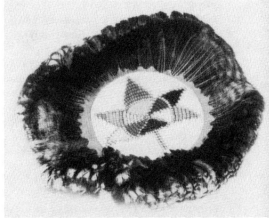

perched on its remaining foot in a nearby tree, seeming little disturbed by the harsh treatment. I have had reports of at least five other Great Grays caught in traps in Manitoba. In view of the number of trappers working within the range of the Great Gray Owl, trapping may be a mortality factor of considerable significance.

Owls, along with hawks and other raptors, have long been persecuted by man for various reasons: as supposed competitors for game or fur, as a hazard to poultry, as natural enemies or easy targets, and for use as trophies. Henderson noted in Alberta: "In 1914, I made a very diligent search for a nest of the Great Gray Owl, exploring every likely piece of timber for several miles around Belvedere, but without success. I saw a couple of birds but was unable to find a nest and almost came to the conclusion that their nesting here in 1913 had been accidental and might not occur again. I think one reason for my failure was the fact that a useless homesteader had located in my best hunting ground and amused himself by killing every owl and hawk he could and tacking them to the side of his shack."

Walter B. Barrows, writing about Michigan birds in 1912, noted: "Judge Steere, of Sault Ste. Marie, tells me that he has seen several specimens [of Great Gray Owls], more or less mutilated, hung up at deer camps in the woods in Chippewa and neighboring counties."

In 1955 Albert Oeming wrote as follows: "Few of North America's most travelled ornithologists have ever seen this continent's largest owl, the handsome Great Gray Owl (Strix nebulosa). Moreover, it is likely that even fewer will be privileged to see it in years to come, for the numbers of this species appear to be diminishing steadily.

"Less than twenty-five years ago the bird was not uncommon in the remote woods of Northern Alberta and throughout the rest of Northern Canada. When the coat of the Red Squirrel began to be used for fur, however, the situation changed suddenly and radically. This addition to the fur list led to the invasion of the great spruce forests of Northern Alberta by thousands of trappers. Since most trappers are imbued with a universal prejudice against owls, believing that all of them prey heavily on fur-bearing animals such as squirrels and so seriously reduce the potential profits of trapping, the Great Gray Owl was condemned along with the ubiquitous Great Horned Owl. As the Great Gray does not have the wary and suspicious nature of the latter species, it made an easy target for trappers' guns. Its decline in numbers was alarmingly swift. . . ."

Heaviest mortality occurs to Great Gray Owls during their irregular winter incursions south and east of their main breeding range in Canada. In the winter of 1842–43 seven were collected in Massachusetts. One can guess that in that early period others were killed but not recorded. About six dead ones were "exposed for sale in the Montreal markets" in the winter of 1876, all having been obtained either on Montreal Island or nearby. A "great flight" took place in southern Ontario and southwestern Quebec in 1889–90; as was typical of those days, many were shot for trophies, forty-nine being handled by two persons. The following winter a taxidermist in eastern Maine received twenty-seven dead ones. In the winter of 1922–23 Winnipeg was invaded by Great Grays; later, columnist Harold Mossop wrote that "numbers were shot by irresponsible gunners." A local birder who was active during that period recalled that after a Winnipeg taxidermist died, his stock of mounted birds was sold at an auction. There were a number of raptors in the collection, including several Great Gray Owls that were sold for twenty-five cents each!

During the winter of 1950–51 a taxidermist at Swastika in northern Ontario received thirty-six dead Great Grays by the end of January. An invasion in southeastern Manitoba and Minnesota in the winter of 1968–69 probably involved more than a hundred birds, as many as twenty reaching the Minneapolis-St. Paul area. Of twenty-four dead owls recorded that season in Manitoba, at least thirteen had been shot. For Minnesota, Janet C. Green noted: "many of the owls died before they were able to make the return journey." The following winter, numbers of Great Grays appeared in northern Minnesota; I found remains of eleven dead ones, more

than half of which had been shot. In 1972 an Alberta observer, William E. McKay, wrote: "A freshly killed Great Gray Owl was found along a road this winter near Rocky Mountain House. Whoever shot it took the time to cut off both legs and took them as trophies but left the owl near where it fell on the snow."

A heavy toll of wintering owls also is taken by collision with motor vehicles. Great Gray Owls fly low across even busy highways, ignoring passing vehicles, gliding slowly, clearly unaware of any danger. Apologetic drivers have brought in dead or crippled owls that flew into their vehicles "as if they were blind." One owl standing on the shoulder of a highway was struck and killed by a snowplow, much to the astonishment of the operator, who had expected the big bird to fly away.

From 1970 to 1979 I recorded forty-three dead owls in our area (not including the eleven I found shot or car-killed in adjacent Minnesota in early spring 1970). Of these, twenty-three were vehicle-collision casualties, four died of unknown causes, two were predated, two were electrocuted, one died after being caught on a barbed-wire fence, and twelve had been shot. One can assume that others were shot and carried away by aspiring taxidermists or trophy seekers. There is a recent report of an owl having been electrocuted in Alberta; after talking to Manitoba and Winnipeg Hydro-Electric employees about two found in our area in 1979, I am convinced that the toll from this source is higher than these few records suggest. Birds accidentally electrocuted on transmission lines are not as likely to be found as birds that die on highways.

Thanks to an enlightened and cooperative public and field staff of the Manitoba Department of Natural Resources, nearly all Great Gray Owls found dead in the province have been obtained by us for use as scientific study skins. These specimens, which have been positively identified to sex, have provided extremely useful information, and are permanently available for further study. Although the preparation of a study skin takes time (about three hours each, as I discovered in the course of preparing more than a dozen in the winter of 1978–79), the benefit to be derived from the specimen far outweighs its use as a mounted bird in someone's home.

Loss of owls through starvation and collision with vehicles can't be controlled, but shooting, which is still an important mortality factor affecting Great Gray Owls, needs to be eliminated. In many regions, despite legal protection, birds of prey are still being shot, either in righteous defense of game species, out of idle curiosity, or through ignorance. Present laws are relatively new, myths are difficult to overcome, and hawks and owls are relatively easy targets. Moreover, magistrates and others who rule on prosecutions, not knowing the value of raptors, often levy only minor fines. If hawks and owls were as numerous as grouse, perhaps it wouldn't matter so much. Ruffed Grouse populations, for example, are little affected by hunting, though hundreds of thousands are shot annually, for they are an abundant species with high reproductive rates. Except in cyclic lows, one can expect to find them everywhere in suitable habitat. Birds of prey, however, being on top of a food chain, are scarce, have low reproductive rates, and some are now rare.

For many people a hawk or owl is a wonderful creature, an element of the wild. But not for all. Everyone thrills to see a deer, but predatory birds generally don't seem to be admired in the same way. The words "predator" and "predatory" in themselves suggest a fearsome creature and an unpleasant kind of behavior. This partly relates to a misunderstanding of the role of the predator. A sentimental view of predation, colored by an unwarranted sympathy for the prey species, whether mouse or chickadee,

merely adds further weight to the myth. Just as the wolf has for so long been thought of as big and bad, so hawks and owls and other raptors have been looked upon as harmful and even evil. For many people there is something repugnant about one warm-blooded vertebrate animal killing another, an act considered much less acceptable than predation on butterflies or earthworms.

Herman J. Brown, a poultry farmer with lots of experience with avian predators, summed up his feelings about them in 1953: "It is well for everyone to know the capacity of these birds for harm, but I don't wish to give the impression that I am in any sense their enemy, or that any poultry grower should act against them without cause. During the years I spent alone [on a farm in northern Wisconsin] they and other animals were my chief source of mental stimulation and entertainment. No one with that experience could feel anything but an abiding friendship for them. Those Goshawks! In retrospect, the image of their savage perfection is worth a good many chickens."

Sportswriters and gun dealers, unfortunately, continue to refer to unprotected animals as vermin, using the terms "varmints" and "varmint-guns," thus extending the notion that animals are either good or bad. In the dictionary, however, "vermin" applies to any "mammals and birds injurious to game, crops, etc." This old definition hardly works any longer, for sportsmen are gradually learning the value of wolf predation on deer and are more than willing to pay the cost of grain eaten by Mallards. Despite this evolution of thought, however, many sportsmen still are reluctant to give up grouse to feed Goshawks, for so long have these and other raptors been identified as targets for "plinking."

Sportsmen also must learn that it is no longer fashionable to display mounted hawks or owls as trophies or decorations in dens. Now that raptors are protected there is no more reason for hanging them on our walls than songbirds or gulls. A mounted bird in a museum case or in a conservation exhibit has educational value. But the hawk, owl, or eagle displayed as a trophy is an anomaly, an artifact of the past. Today in Manitoba (and until 1979 in Ontario), in order to have a raptor mounted legally a permit must first be obtained, and a permit is issued only when it can be shown that the specimen will be used for educational purposes. Even if a person finds a dead hawk or owl (or claims to have found it), he is unable to have it preserved legally for private use. Thus, another incentive for shooting raptors has been removed.

Reducing illegal shooting is one step; getting hunters to appreciate and enjoy hawks and owls and other raptors is perhaps more important. This educational task should begin in the classroom. The task is of turning hunters into hunter-naturalists. Convincing a hunter to buy his first bird book may be worth more than selling a second one to a confirmed birder. Hunters need to realize that learning to recognize raptors is more fun and a better challenge than using them for targets. Being actively involved with wildlife and the outdoors, and often engaged in efforts to increase and maintain wildlife habitat, hunters are all potential naturalists. With binoculars and bird books so readily available, an additional feature of the sportsman's day afield may yet include watching hawks and owls.

Interest in rehabilitation of injured raptors has increased in recent years, with several centers or individuals now receiving birds from various sources. Those that can be brought to a state of normality are released; permanently disabled birds are kept for propagation purposes (with progeny being released to the wild), or turned over to zoos. Three injured Great Gray Owls have been turned over by us to the Owl Rehabilitation Research Foundation at Vineland, Ontario. To ensure the safe journey of the first of these, an adult female owl with a broken wing, Mrs. Katherine ("Kay") McKeever of the Vineland center flew to Winnipeg. After several phone calls and considerable discussion with Department of Transport Officials, staff of the Winnipeg International Airport, and the flight crew of a major airline, permission was granted to take the bird on board the jet plane. Kay then changed her ticket to first class (because that section was empty), and bought a colorful baby sleeper outfit in which she tucked the owl. After carefully covering its face with a pink blanket, Kay boarded the plane, assisted by a stewardess. I have often wondered what the reaction would have been had any interested person between Winnipeg and Toronto lifted the blanket to look at the baby.

9

A Time of Change

On cold February mornings, frost-laden air lies heavy over the land. Against the early light of dawn every branch, every twig glistens with frost crystals. Old owl nests lie silent in the warped crowns of tamarack trees, exposed to any prying eyes. Though there is little protection from wind, snow, and cold in such a nest, this does not deter Great Gray Owls, who may be crouching upon eggs in a nest in mid-March. Crackling cold temperatures test the adaptations of this species to weather at northern latitudes.

Despite the low temperatures, the owls unknowingly respond to changing daylength, and certain behavior gradually changes, too. The male, instead of immediately swallowing a captured mouse, carries it to a nearby perch and sits motionless, staring quietly, prey hanging from its bill. It is a tantalizing sight for the female. Drawn to the same feeding grounds and perhaps competing for food, engaged for long periods in nocturnal bouts of hooting with each other and others of their kind, the pair has for several months reacted to each other aggressively and cautiously.

The sight of the dangling mouse releases in the female an ancient pattern—a curious mimicry of a hungry, young owl—shifting her weight deliberately from one foot to the other, bobbing her head and hooting softly, she begins chirping like an owlet. The male is mesmerized by this performance, hearing a sound he has not heard since attending a nest eight months earlier. He sits, watching closely as she flies toward him and lands on a nearby perch. Now they are closer than they have been all fall and winter. After some hesitation, for she is larger than he is, stimulated by the female's continued display, the male flies to perch beside her, closing his eyes as he leans toward her, holding out the mouse. With closed eyes and a slight mewing sound the female seizes the mouse. At the moment the female takes the mouse from the male the pair bond is formed or renewed.

The ritual of courtship feeding will be repeated again and again, strengthening the social bond. Many days will pass before there are eggs in a nest, but this crucial behavior determines their new relationship.

Pair formation, courtship, mating, and territoriality are among the least documented aspects of Great Gray Owl behavior. Earlier observations, although sporadic, indicated the existence of a considerable repertoire. In the past two years, especially, observations of captive and wild birds have helped to build a substantial, though yet incomplete, story of what happens. There is now evidence that aerial displays, mutual preening, and courtship feeding occur in this species.

Occasionally, in February and March, we have seen a Great Gray Owl capture a vole and then, departing from the usual pattern of winter feeding in which prey is eaten as soon as captured, carry it away in its bill and sit idly on a perch for a minute or two before feeding. This may be one of the first overt signs of breeding behavior in the male. Some time between January and April, pair formation and courtship take place. During this period the male feeds the female, thus establishing a close relationship with her.

In the Snowy Owl the sight of the male carrying a lemming provides stimulation leading to nesting behavior. As the courting male approaches with a lemming in its bill, according to Philip Taylor, it moves in a slow, undulating flight with wings raised in a V over the back. Parmelee has suggested that the number of available lemmings, and the rate at which the male can bring them to the female, work in some obscure fashion to initiate nesting and even to determine the number of eggs that the female lays! "When lemmings are abundant, the male places a goodly number of his catch beneath a favorite perch. Although we have never witnessed this piling up of lemmings by the male before the female, we have seen the evidence—upwards of a dozen uneaten lemmings scattered on the ground below a perch. At one perch we counted 26 lemmings in one heap!"

When small mammals abound, Great Gray Owls do well, raising large families

and tolerating others of their own kind as well as other raptor species at close range. In such years they may lay as many as nine eggs, though a clutch of four is about average.

Perhaps, as in the Snowy Owl, the female Great Gray Owl is stimulated to lay a larger clutch by the frequency with which the male brings prey; up to six dead voles have been found lying on the edge of an active nest. It also has been theorized that courtship feeding has important nutritive value; during the period in which the eggs are developing, the female's energy requirements are greater than the male's.

When mice or voles are scarce, only one or two eggs may be laid, or the birds may not nest at all. If there should be a shortage of food after the eggs have hatched, then the growth rate of the young may be greatly reduced and some chicks may perish. The rapid growth rate of nestlings under normal development requires an abundant food supply. Höglund and Lansgren have shown that five days after hatching, a young owl may have tripled its weight and at two weeks of age may reach five hundred grams, from about forty grams at hatching.

Great Gray Owls demonstrate their interdependence in nesting as well as food habits. They habitually choose an abandoned or vacant nest built by another species, hence their nests vary in size, location, and condition. In our region, Common Crow, Common Raven, Red-tailed Hawk, and Broad-winged Hawk nests are probably most frequently used. The height of nests occupied by Great Gray Owls ranges from eight to sixty-five feet above ground; in Scandinavia, nests have been found on low stumps and even on the ground. Despite published statements to the contrary, there is no evidence of which I am aware that Great Gray Owls add any nest material.

Unlike the eggs of most owls, which are round, the chalk-white eggs of Great

Grays are decidedly ovoid or conical, a characteristic perhaps of some advantage when laying in old, well-used nests that sometimes have an unyielding, level surface. For a bird of the size of the Great Gray Owl, the egg is surprisingly small, being a little more than two inches in length and noticeably less in width, not even as large as a hen's egg.

Probably some time prior to breeding, one or more nest structures, perhaps one used by the pair in a previous year, become focal points for their activities. We have evidence that Great Grays visit nests as early as mid-February, at least in mild winters in this region. Since egg-laying may begin here in mid-March or earlier, it should be no surprise to find birds looking over potential nest sites a few weeks in advance. Nest-searching behavior was observed by Henderson in west-central Alberta on March 19, 1915. Shortly before dark he found a bird in a nest and another perched nearby. The bird in the nest "made a deep booming sound and the one on the limb a kind of whistle. After about a minute the one on the nest flew away and its mate followed. . . . The Owls had not yet decided which nest they would use. They were merely house-hunting."

On April 20, 1974, Spencer Sealy and I found a pair of owls in the vicinity of two nests a few hundred feet apart. The female was bolder than the male and remained perched near the larger of the nests. Initially disappointed not to see her at this nest four days later, we found her instead in the second nest, lying low and motionless as if on eggs. We returned a few minutes later with tree-climbing spurs, but she was gone, and the nest was empty. Four days later we were even more surprised to find her sitting in the first nest incubating two fresh eggs!

Although the male may play an important role in finding nests, the female probably makes the final choice. Höglund and Lansgren noted of Great Gray Owls in Sweden: "To all appearances, the owls visit various nests and finally they decide upon one of them. The male calls at the nest, but it seems that the female is the one determining whether or not the nest can be approved. At the time of our visit [end of April 1961] none of the great gray owls had laid their eggs. Yet they were staying in the neighborhood of the nests, and some of them were even observed in the nests."

Defense of territories appears minimal, some Great Grays in Sweden, for example, showing a surprising tolerance and nesting as close together as a hundred meters. Possibly this depends on rodent abundance. When prey is scarce, the male may search for hours over a wide area. Maximum diameter of the range at a nest in Wyoming, as reported by the Craighead brothers, was one and a quarter miles. Where prey is locally abundant the male may find all he needs within a half-mile or less of the nest. Selection of a nest seems to be based in part on the presence of high prey population. Aggressive encounters on winter feeding grounds, in some cases far from breeding sites, may be understood partly in terms of competition for food. Since sexual behavior in this species begins early in the season, however, encounters in late February and March may have some sexual connection. On February 24, 1974, when we forced an owl to move back into a woods, a marked female sitting up high and watching about a hundred yards away at once flew toward it and they grappled, hitting feet together in midair. This was within a few hundred yards of a nest later occupied by the attacking female. A half hour before sunset at another locality a few weeks later, two birds, first seen flying about in wide circles, approached each other in an apparently aggressive manner. One made a pass at the other and then flew up above it. They briefly came together, tussled in midair, and tumbled down to the snow before flying off in separate directions.

We have heard and seen females soliciting males by begging for food, and on a few occasions the male of a pair has been seen capturing prey and then flying off with it while accompanying or following the female into woods. Two examples follow: On March 18, 1979, we watched a pair of birds actively hunting in bright light from 6:15 to 10:00 a.m. Neither responded to any of our lures; they seemed too engrossed in each other to pay any attention to us. Once, both birds perched a few feet apart on the cross-arm of a power pole. We returned later that evening and found them back out again, behaving in much the same way. For a long time the male sat on top of a pole, occasionally glancing down at two live mice in a bal-chatri trap. Then, as if on signal, as the female headed toward the woods, the male casually dropped off his perch, plunged into the snow, and emerged with prey in one foot. He flew directly after the female, both disappearing in approximately the same direction.

Late in the evening on March 24 that same year, we found another pair engaged in similar activity, and equally unresponsive to our lures. Both birds appeared to be actively searching for prey, particularly the male who was busily shifting his head about, scanning the snow. Within a few minutes he dove down, came out of the snow with a vole in his foot, and flew off to perch close beside the female. It looked as if we were about to witness courtship feeding, but they flew off into the woods, the female leading, the male still holding the prey.

On March 2, 1975, Ray Tuokko found a concentration of thirty-three fresh plunge-holes in woods within a quarter-mile or less of an old nest. Three plunge-holes were found close to the nest tree; no plunge-holes were found outside this locality. Apparently, a male, or a pair, had hunted successfully (judging by spots of blood at some holes) for a few days around a potential nest site.

Plunging itself appears to be a part of pair formation or courtship, in some cases being performed as display rather than functional behavior. There were times in late winter, especially, when birds seemed in a frenzy of plunging activity; when overly desperate plunges suggested something more than hunger as motivation.

The entire flight sequence, beginning with soaring out over an open area, hovering, and then at last dropping down into or onto the snow, was seen by us on several occasions under circumstances indicating a display function. We observed an aerial display of this type for the first time on February 19, 1978. A bird, presumed by size and behavior to be a male, was seen on several occasions in December 1977 on the edge of a woods adjacent to farmland. It was the same vicinity, if not the same tree, where a male had regularly perched in late winter 1974, prior to occupying a nearby nest. The new male was shy and retreated each time a car approached. As we neared it, the bird flew into the woods and out of sight. We parked about a hundred yards away and, as an experiment, I played a tape recording of the begging call of a female owl, one kept by me briefly the previous November. Almost immediately the male came back out. Upon my repeating the tape, the bird twice flew slowly over an open field in level flight, wings atilt. Without pausing it turned and slowly flew back onto its perch. Two or three times it looked back into the woods, even though the tape was still running. Later I glimpsed a second bird, presumably a female. I am convinced that the female begging call had elicited courtship display in a territorial male.

It is not always easy to tell whether a bird is seeking prey or just going through the motions. On one occasion, we had two owls in sight. One bird (the female?) had forced the other (the male?) out into an open area. The bird in the open acted, in some respects, as if it were hunting, flying out over the meadow, hovering, and then dropping down onto the snow, but it

did this in a casual manner. When the bird performed a third or fourth time closer to us (and not coincidentally closer to the first bird), landing on a paved road, the display function became clear. The owl took a few steps as if searching for prey, then hopped up onto blocks of frozen snow on the edge of the road, peering and leaning forward excitedly as if it had prey in sight. The first owl, still in sight, clearly was the stimulus object, for when it flew away, the bird on the road in front of us flew off after it!

On March 3, 1979, two owls came chasing after the cast lure at about the same time. This led to a brief antagonistic flurry between the two competitors, followed by what could only be described as a bout of snow-plunging. The next day, despite the advantage of three witnesses to interpret actions of three owls in sight, we still were puzzled by events of a similar nature. It was an exceedingly bright, mild afternoon. Things began to get complicated when I cast the lure for the nearest bird. Its approach was cut short by a second, more distant bird that came in faster and drove the first bird off. The two circled above us in a brief flurry of broad, flapping wings, a silent, spectacular clash. Seconds later, the harassed bird (I thought, but not all agreed) began rapidly snow-plunging, circling, hovering, and dropping in casual, random fashion, hardly with any time to detect prey. Soon two, and then all three birds were doing this. None

An owl's preening response to a human head is shown in this sequence. As the author's bared head is lowered and presented to the owl, the bird (top to bottom) tilts its head sideways in readiness to preen; owl in tilt!; preening in process—owl nibbling base of hairs; and pulling (usually gently!) on a few strands.

seemed serious about catching anything, at times merely dropping onto the snow, then looking about as if to see what the others were doing. We had difficulty keeping track of the birds' identities as they circled and crossed each other's paths, and we couldn't be sure of the sexes. Still, it was a moment of splendid confusion. It seemed evident that this was pseudo-hunting behavior, whether functioning as courtship, appeasement, or territoriality.

One of the most detailed observations of pair interaction was made late in the evening of March 11, 1978, by Ray Tuokko. He had observed a male and female on three weekends hunting in an area of open fields surrounded by aspen and mixed-wood forest. A slightly revised version of part of his notes follows:

The female, hunting in one field, caught a rodent after five minutes' observation. She continued hunting for ten minutes, flying in large circles or completely across the field, hovering and plunging. She then flew to trees near a road, and the male was noticed approaching from the opposite end of the field. He perched in a tree some distance from her, whereupon she flew toward him. He flew out to meet her as she neared his perch and "he chased her around the tree twice, then both landed in the same tree, with the female 10 feet lower and on the opposite side of the tree. They remained there about 10 minutes, occasionally shifting position. The male occasionally bowed and tipped his tail up as if he were anticipating a flight." Both constantly turned their heads in all directions as if listening to some unseen bird, or possibly responding to the observer.

Next, the female left her perch, immediately pursued by the male. "They proceeded in a spiral, flapping flight of about 20 to 30 feet in diameter. They circled about in this manner, gaining about 40 to 50 feet altitude. . . . I could hear their wings touching noisily during the flight, but there was no body contact. This flight was terminated by a steep descent to nearby trees." At this point, partly because of the failing light and distance, the size differences could not be discerned. "They remained perched for about 5 minutes, then commenced an undulating, circular flight amongst the trees, so that *I could hear their wings banging recklessly against branches.*"

A little later Ray moved toward where the birds had disappeared and found an owl he thought was the male. It was very alert and kept turning its head as if listening to distant sounds. The male then flew toward Ray and perched nearby, alternately looking directly at him and in the direction of the female. He thought the male was defending his territory, or at least placing "himself between me and the female."

Based on this extended observation of a pair, the next day (March 12) Ray built a nest nearby in a small spruce-tamarack stand. The nest was successfully occupied by Great Gray Owls that season, likely the courting pair seen by Ray, for no other birds had been using that area. One of three eggs in the nest hatched on May 13, indicating a probable first laying on April 14, just four weeks after the nest was constructed!

Preening is one of the strongest patterns evident in pair bonding behavior for the Great Gray Owl, and can be readily elicited from both sexes, and adults as well as sub-adults. Every grown owl I have tested has shown a strikingly similar response. All I have had to do is to get the bird's attention and then push the top of my head toward its face. This gesture of submission leads the bird to run its bill through my hair, gently nibbling along the scalp and often seizing and pulling on a few hairs. Even badly injured birds have shown this response, but it varies in extent, depending on the individual and circumstances. Usually, as soon as I offer a bird the top or sides of my bare head it at once alters its facial plumage, pulling

back the facial discs, raising the rictal bristles, stretching its neck up to full length, and then tilting its head to one side with partly closed eyes. Then it preens. When it stops and withdraws, the behavior can be elicited again by pushing my head against its face. Between preening bouts it often maintains the whole peculiar attitude, in the extreme position holding its head tipped sideways. Usually the pupils are constricted.

It also frequently bumps its bill against my head and occasionally I return the favor, repeatedly bumping my nose against its bill. Even aggressive birds can be treated in this fashion—and I am convinced that this helps reduce their aggressiveness—although a recent nose bite has led to some restraint in my bill-to-bill encounters.

In 1954 Al Oeming observed preening in a pair of captive Great Gray Owls: "The male would fly to the female's stump and face her. Standing face to face with breasts touching, he would commence rubbing his beak over hers, at the same time uttering a faint droning or humming sound. Often he would circle her face with his beak in a similar manner. This was observed regularly for eight days and would occur at any time during the day or night." Recently, similar behavior was reported in the related Barred Owl; in the summer of 1972, John W. Fitzpatrick witnessed and photographed mutual preening or "allopreening" in two wild birds. As reported by him in an ornithological journal; "Most preening was directed at the edges of the facial discs and the feathers surrounding the bill. . . . Periodically owl A gave thin, high-pitched notes reminiscent of those of a small dog while preening and, more consistently, while being preened. . . . Allopreening . . . appears to function as a means of sex recognition in some monomorphic species, and it may, in addition, provide a ritualized mechanism for pair bond maintenance in species that pair for extended periods."

Signs of pair formation: male on the left, female on the right. Note the compressed plumage of the male and the fluffed plumage of the female. A few minutes later, the male caught a vole and, carrying it in his bill, followed the female into the woods.

The functions of allopreening were recently reviewed by Eric Forsman and Howard Wight. Their study, which included observations of this behavior in the closely related Spotted Owl, led them to suggest that allopreening is ritualized aggressive pecking or biting, appearing as a peaceful interaction between individuals.

Following a fortuitous irruption in late winter 1978–79 of Great Gray Owls into the Ottawa area far from known breeding grounds, preening was observed for the first time in the wild. Richard M. Poulin, an ornithologist at the National Museum of Canada, kindly consented to let me publish this key observation. As reported by him, by late February pairing seemed to have occured in some of these displaced birds. On February 27 at least four apparent pairs were observed, two pairs being in the same tree. Of these latter, one pair kept in "very close proximity to each other . . . [they] were seen to bend towards each other until they were noticeably horizontal. In this position they were seen to preen each other about the face and head. The smaller male bird was most active. . . . This preening and caressing . . . lasted between 15 and 20 minutes. We could detect no sounds associated with this behavior. . . . The preening occurred between 8 and 9 a.m. The weather was warm (2° C) with heavy overcast and flurries, little wind."

Highly perceptive and significant observations of preening (or grooming) and courtship feeding have been made of a pair of captive Great Gray Owls by Katherine McKeever at the Vineland, Ontario, Owl Rehabilitation Research Foundation. The female owl was a one-winged amputee from Manitoba (for *that* story see the last paragraph in Chapter 8, p. 100), in residence with Kay and her husband, Larry, since March 1977. Otherwise in excellent health, the owl moved about her sumptuous quarters by walking along a series of long perches. The male, a bird from Moosonee, Ontario, recovering from

trap-injured feet, was introduced into a large, outdoor cage in late December 1977. In early February 1978, when the male had recovered sufficiently so that he could feed himself, the female was put in with the male. Kay's notes (spring 1978) are so marvelously descriptive that I have used almost her entire letter:

"Initially—that is, for about two days!— she was surprisingly aggressive towards him but on the morning of the third day I was astounded to see them sitting side by side—wings almost touching—and both looking as if they had ALWAYS sat together that way! It was later in the afternoon of the same day that I saw them grooming each other, the male making the first moves and sticking the top of his facial discs toward her at the level of her mandibles, with his eyes closed. She would lean towards him a little and groom the edges of his discs, with her eyes closed too. Then she would often groom herself, following this (or preceding it) by stropping her beak on the perch as if to wipe something off it!

"Later (i.e., several days) he grew bolder and would fly to her and groom her first, then bowing his head and inviting her to groom him. When they had been together for about two weeks, it seemed to me that if they weren't dozing they were grooming! He would lift one of her feet in his talons, without apparently throwing her off balance, and nibble at it gently—much in the same way that I have seen owls nibbling at their own toes, as if cleaning the base of the talons. Even though her foot was thus held out and up at a slightly awkward (to human eyes) angle to her roosting body, she usually kept her eyes closed. Sometimes she would chitter a little and he would then let go, so I took the chitter to be a mild protest.

"Another grooming action that I saw three or four times was the male 'combing' the breast feathers of the female with the talons of one foot. At such times, their bodies were turned towards each

other on the pole perches, whereas in the foot-lifting and grooming routine, the female remained perched with her left flank to the male.

"I cannot say which one usually initiated the facial grooming because when I looked at them they were either asleep or already at it! However, from my observations it was almost always the male who flew to the female, if they were on different poles, and at such times he would approach her and make the first advances, usually by stretching out his face to her, with eyes closed, and either be groomed or nibble at her discs. On the other hand, she groomed him much longer than he groomed her, and at such times they were very close—side breast to side breast—and he seemed to have telescoped his body down to a very low height, eyes tightly closed, plumage half fluffed, while she towered over him, nibbling at the top of his head, the back of his head, his face and side neck and around his mandibles and ears. Often this was accompanied by contented little sighs and grunts, although

I couldn't tell from which owl they came—perhaps from both.

"In April (13th) I saw him up on the pole adjoining her favourite pole, with a mouse dangling from his mouth. He would put it down, hold it on the perch with one foot, pause, take it in his beak again, turn around a few times, look around (it didn't seem to me, specifically AT her) and put it back under his foot again. Eventually he would eat it, sometimes on the spot, sometimes flying off with it. Four days later I watched him lodge the mouse, with some care, at the confluence of the two poles and go away and leave it. I never saw her take it but it always was gone in about an hour's time. On April 19th he ran back and forth along her pole and the adjoining one, with the mouse hanging from his beak and FINALLY went right up to her and thrust out the mouse, eyes closed. She turned her head on the side so her beak was at right angles to his and closed her eyes as she touched the mouse.

"There was quite a bit of vocalization

At some time during the courtship period a nest is visited by the pair. The female sits on the nest for a few days, and may visit more than one nest.

in the preamble to the food transfer, almost all from him. It was a soft, low, series of one-note rapid hoots. Does she make this noise to remind him of the noise he makes when he brings it, thus triggering his action, or is there a paucity of available noises, and this one means bringing food—whether asking for it or offering it??? I haven't heard the female Great Gray Owl make this noise yet, but she hasn't been on eggs yet, or fed young.

"By April 23rd the male dangled the mouse and the female came to HIM and took it. By April 27th she came right to the platform where he sat and took the mouse. Later that evening I saw her pick up a mouse that was draped over the platform edge, and eat it. I have to assume that he put it there, although to my amazement, on the 28th, I saw *her* down at the food box taking a mouse for herself, and walking up one of the ascending limbs with it dangling from HER beak, and then saw HER tuck it into the niche of the two poles!! Meanwhile, HE sat on one pole and stared into space! Suffering mackerel!"

The act of mating has rarely been observed in the Great Gray Owl. Our only record is a brief observation made on March 27, 1971. The event took place in late afternoon during a light snowfall. We had searched unsuccessfully all day for owls, then suddenly saw one on the tip of a tall spruce near a farm house. A few minutes later it moved to a wooded creekbed near the road and began hunting. I approached it as it sat on a tree stump about twelve feet high. When I was within twenty feet of the bird, which turned out to be a female, she turned about, glared at me and aggressively snapped her bill several times before flying away. Later she was joined by a second bird, apparently her mate. The pair flew off together to an open field and just out of our sight. Hurriedly climbing on top of the car for a view, we saw the female (recognizable by a broken wing

feather) perched about fifteen feet above the snow on the tip of a dead, leaning tamarack pole with the male astride her, vigorously flapping his wings. At the same time, one or both birds gave a peculiar, rasping screech, audible though we were more than three hundred yards away. Shortly thereafter the male flew away and the female resumed hunting. Observers in Sweden heard copulating Great Grays give a "series of squeaking notes."

On February 28, 1978, conservation officer Ken de Graff observed owls in a sexual encounter about fifty feet away through the window of his home at Wabowden, 340 miles north of Winnipeg. This incident happened between 6:00 and 6:30 p.m. A pair of Great Gray Owls, which had been observed nearby for at least a week, were seen moving from one telephone pole to another. The male, which always flew first, then landed on the house, whereupon the dog barked at it. The male next flew into a tree, where shortly he was joined by the female. At that point the birds were about twenty feet apart on the same branch, with the female perched ten feet higher than the male. When the female flew, the male followed and, like a Raven, cupped his wings, braking and falling upon her in midair. The male dropped onto the female for a second; then they separated and flew off together. Nothing like this has previously been reported for this species. Presumably this was an established pair, the aerial contact indicating a strong sexual motivation by the male.

We have found fresh feathers in nests visited by owls from mid-February into May. Prior to egg-laying, a female may visit more than one nest, accidentally losing several feathers, making us uncertain which nest she is going to choose. This habit seems so common, we think the presence of two or three nests built in close proximity provides additional nesting stimulus. Since Great Gray Owls begin laying as early as mid-March, when

temperatures are frequently low, the insulative quality of plumage is important in keeping eggs warm. The female's well-developed brood patch is the source of heat. This bare, highly vascularized area, from which a handful of feathers have been shed, is about three and a half inches wide, extending from the upper breast and shoulder region to the vent. A thin layer of feathers, drawn from the developing brood patch, sometimes lies beneath the eggs and may provide some insulation.

Maintaining eggs at close to ninety-eight degrees Fahrenheit, when the temperature may be as much as thirty or forty degrees below zero, also requires close sitting. The persistent attendance of the female is a behavioral trait of significance to successful incubation. Unlike waterfowl, the females of which surround their eggs with down and other nest material when they leave the nest, there is no covering for owl eggs, nor hardly any opportunity to fly off from brood responsibilities.

The incubation period for a Great Gray Owl egg is about thirty days, but the period from laying of the first egg to hatching of the last egg laid may be from thirty to fifty days, depending on the size of the clutch and the interval at which eggs are laid. We found an egg-laying interval of three days, but it is reported by others to range from three days to an extreme of twelve.

For two and a half months, from the moment the first egg is laid, through incubation and development of the nestlings, the female is on or at the nest. Depending on weather and temperature, she may sit on the nest for twenty-four hours daily, despite snow and cold, wind and rain. When her offspring are able to maintain their own body temperature, she may leave them once a day for a few minutes respite. To keep up the female's strength and energy, to keep eggs and nestlings heated, and the latter fed, the male must bring a copious supply of food to the nest. Each day he must capture prey to feed the rapidly growing young, as well as his mate and himself. Before the young are two weeks old he may be bringing a dozen or more voles daily.

The male owl's diligence in hunting and bringing prey, no less than the attentiveness of his mate, is evidence of the continuing strength of the pair bond. The relationship that began in late winter, arising out of mutual preening, courtship feeding, and mating, provides family stability that lasts through summer and into autumn.

10
A Nesting of Owls

At dawn in early summer in the spruce woods, singing birds produce a medley of sounds as pervasive and constant as a running brook. Murmurs, whistles, lisping conversational notes, ringing musical tones intermingle as patterned light beams through mist and boughs. Each stirring song proclaims a new day.

In the midst of these sounds a soft, mellow hooting comes from high in a tamarack. In the rising orange light, a female Great Gray Owl slowly pivots her head toward a distant grove, then calls again, without opening her bill, giving three measured hoots. The downy head of a nestling owl pushes up beside her, chirping anxiously, hungrily tossing its head back, its bill open. Out of the deep shadows comes a gliding form; on set wings the male owl slips across an opening in the trees, suddenly rising abruptly to perch on the tip of a slender snag. The female watches intently, motionless, as the male bends its head down to pick up a mouse held in one foot. A moment later the male springs forward, flaps its wings heavily, then steadily glides toward the nest tree. He swoops upward effortlessly, his momentum carrying him precisely to the edge of the nest, mouse swinging in his bill. With no change of expression, the female leans toward the male and seizes the mouse, both closing their eyes at the moment of contact. A moment later the male turns and plunges off the nest, gliding rapidly away through the forest.

Though the young owls bob and weave about, pushing out from under her wings and breast, the female methodically snips open the mouse, holding it with one foot, then eats the stringy entrails. Using her bill, she delicately feeds bits of bright flesh to one or more of the owlets until the mouse is consumed.

The sounds of other busy birds still ring in the forest, but now the owls are quiet; the female shuffles about, adjusting herself upon the nestlings. Calmly turning to face the sun, now bright above the ragged spruce tops, she blinks several times, settles lower onto the nest, closes her eyes to slits, and is still.

In earlier days Great Gray Owls and their nests or eggs were often collected as soon as they were discovered. One of the first nests found in the United States, together with three fresh eggs, was sold by Henry Halvorson, a trapper, to amateur ornithologist Per O. Fryklund for three dollars. The nest was discovered in northwestern Minnesota less than a mile from the Canadian border on April 4, 1935.

In those days of ornithological exploration, naturalists with collections like Fryklund's were contributing to knowledge of birds. Museums were building scientific collections and specimens were in great demand. Fryklund paid Halvorson a dollar for each Great Gray Owl he shot, about ten being taken by the latter from this area over several years. A bird shot on April 25, 1926, had a well-developed brood patch, suggesting the bird had been incubating. In 1933 Fryklund found enlarged ova in another bird. Thereafter, he had urged Halvorson to try to find a Great Gray Owl nest.

When we visited Henry Halvorson in 1975, though it was forty years since he had found the nest, and he was seventy-three years old, he still clearly recalled the event. As he explained, in those depression years three dollars was a considerable sum. Halvorson, who had been making his living from trapping, set out that early April day on skis to check his traps. As he approached a grove of mixed conifers, two agitated owls flew out to meet him. He soon found their nest, which was about ten feet above ground, in some closely grown tamaracks. Both birds attacked him when he climbed up to get the nest, flapping their wings about him, hooting, and plucking at his hat. Carefully placing the nest and eggs in his packsack, he then skied away, followed for a short distance by the owls.

Sitting in the Halvorson home, looking at photos of Henry as a youthful trapper standing in front of a cabin draped with pelts of wolves, fox, and mink, gave us some insight into the period of that earlier nesting. Listening to his account of the event, we briefly shared in the discovery. We also talked about a more recent discovery, a second nest found only about five miles east of his nest site and studied by us in 1970.

My attention was drawn to this area by a Winnipeg physician, Henry T. Dirks, who reported seeing eight live Great Gray Owls along a two-mile stretch of highway on April 1, 1970. Owls had evidently been attracted here during the winter by an abundance of voles. Unfortunately, a heavy toll was taken by shooting and collision with vehicles; over the next several weeks I found the remains of nine owls. Since some of these had died much earlier than the eight reported by my informant, there may have been two dozen or more owls in this vicinity. Two were salvaged as museum specimens, but the others were worthless. Soggy and dismembered, their remains were a sorry sight. On my first visit to the area on April 11, I saw a dark, moving form in a distant tree that I was sure was an owl. So it was, but an old, dead one, caught on a branch, one wing hanging down and flapping pathetically in the breeze.

Logging operations adjacent to the highway during the winter just past had left a large clearing in which a few tall tamaracks remained. One of these, not more than a hundred yards from the edge of the highway, held a large, conspicuous nest. Since I had just found three dead owls and hadn't seen a live one, I gave the nest only a cursory glance. A few days later, to my disbelief, customs officer Clarence Nordstrom phoned to say "a big owl" was sitting on that same nest. That weekend Bob Taylor and I drove to the site and, even before we stopped our car, we could see the large head of a Great Gray Owl on the nest!

We sat for some time, enthusiastic at seeing our second Great Gray nest, but worried about its survival. The nest, about

This nest and its occupant—high in a tamarack tree in April—could readily be seen from an adjacent busy highway. Goshawks probably built the nest the incubating owl is using.

thirty-five feet up in a tree that had few branches, was exposed to the elements as well as to every passing motorist. The logged-over area seemed bleak compared to the distant groves of spruce and tamarack; in all, the nest site seemed a poor choice. Later, we contacted customs officers on both sides of the border, explaining the value of this nesting, and with their cooperation established a watch on the nest. At our request, the local conservation officer spoke with those people thought to be responsible for the shooting during the previous months, and he also regularly patrolled the area. Eventually, numerous local people became aware of the nest and our interest in its welfare. The generally protective attitude that

soon developed surely helped save the nest.

A phone call in early May to Dalton Muir in Ottawa, telling him about the nest, brought immediate action. Although Muir had photographed many kinds of owls, the Great Gray was a species he had seen only as a rare winter visitant. Taking a leave of absence from his job, in a few days he was in Winnipeg with a trailer loaded with a wooden, portable observation tower. A little later, with Herb Copland's assistance, a forty-foot tower was erected within ten feet of the nest tree. The incubating female proved to be imperturbable, remaining on the nest during construction of the tower. When a small branch blocking the photographer's view

of the nest was sawed off, the female tugged vigorously at the saw blade with her bill, without leaving the nest! It was soon found that the blind was unnecessary; the female paid us little attention, and the male brought food despite our obvious presence. At times the persistent photographer even had to prod the nest with a pole to make the relaxed female open her eyes. We were at the nest site on twenty-two days between May 2 and July 29. Muir was there for the longest period, living in a tent in the bog, photographing owls day and night.

From the vantage point of the tower, perched level with the nest and less than ten feet away, we sat face to face with the mother owl. We could also study details of the food exchange. The male's delivery of prey was fast and direct; swooping up

the edge of the nest, landing hard on his usual perch, he seemed always impatient to depart. Often, before he had folded his wings he was offering prey to the female. Both closed their eyes briefly when the female took the food from his bill.

Muir observed that "the female, in order to grasp the food, turned her head sideways and delicately took the carcass. Only when the hen had a firm grip and pulled, did the male release his grip. The sideways grip of the female appeared necessary to the successful transfer of the food, because several times the female attempted to grasp the mouse without turning her head and each time the transfer was awkward or the mouse was dropped altogether." Sometimes the female failed to respond at all; then the male, looking about nervously, dropped the prey on the edge of the nest or flew away with it, sometimes perching in a nearby tree and devouring it.

Hatching of the first egg in this nest occurred shortly after the tower was installed. Muir noted that the female was restless and squirming about, in contrast to her former immobility. A "barely perceptible squeaking" from a young bird emerging from an egg was heard at this time. With the hatching of the young, the male brought more food. Though he saw us almost daily, he still remained wary. On some occasions the male's hunting behavior was initiated by calls from the female, and possibly from the young. When not hunting, he was often dozing quietly on a branch, sometimes cocking his head to follow the progress of a nearby vole. On one occasion I watched while he sat in this manner for fifteen minutes. When the female called from the nest, he at once began actively hunting. Moving quickly from perch to perch on low stumps, peering here and there as he moved, within three minutes he captured a meadow vole and hurriedly carried it to the nest.

Voles were abundant in the area and we frequently saw them scurrying about. Little effort seemed required by the male to obtain food, and he mainly hunted within a quarter-mile or less of the nest. Usually, when the male caught prey he flew off, carrying it in one foot. Before flying to the nest, however, he stopped to perch in a tree, landing and balancing easily on one foot, and transferred the vole to his bill. Thus, when he approached the nest, the vole would be dangling from his bill. Peak feeding activities were from 4:30 a.m. to about 8:30 a.m., and from 4:30 p.m. until after dark, but on cloudy days, and sometimes even on bright days, the male might bring food at any time. The midday period, however, was usually an inactive time. Feeding at night was observed with the aid of a large spotlight powered by eight car batteries. Although the bright light lit up the nest and much of the sur-

rounding area, it seemed to have no effect on the birds. During the several times all-night vigils were maintained, the owls were relatively inactive from about 10:30 p.m. to 2:30 a.m. At other nests, when there was a food shortage, we found that the male was forced to hunt at all hours of the day and night.

When the young were small, the female fed them small portions of flesh, but within two weeks they were gulping down whole meadow voles and other rodents. The way in which the young were fed was closely observed by Muir, who reported: "The significance of the sideways turn of the head during food transfer became apparent when the hen fed the young. Small, downy, and blind at first, the young could only extend their heads through the hen's breast feathers, open their mouths and beg with a whimpering squeak. The hen tore off tiny pieces of flesh from the mouse and placed her curved beak directly into the gaping mouth of the young, at right angles to it. On contact with the hen's beak, the young owl clamped its mandibles on each side of the hen's beak and pulled back. Only when this right angle contact was firmly established did the hen relax her grip and allow the young to withdraw the morsel of food. The process was carried out gently, with great patience and evident concern."

Long after the young were good-sized, the female continued to shelter them from the elements. Her persistent attention was well demonstrated one day in June when it rained. The female closed her eyes as the rain increased, hunched lower over the young until she was almost flat on the nest, covering them completely, while drops of water ran down and off the end of her tail. By the time the rain had stopped, her plumage was thoroughly soaked and disarranged. Her head looked like a wet mop, and she shook it several times as vigorously as a dog. Then, with the dry young beginning to squirm out from under her, she stood up and began to preen. By ruffling and shaking her plumage, standing up in the warm breeze and preening her long breast feathers, her plumage was soon restored to normal.

When the young were about three weeks old the nest collapsed, possibly as a result of the growing belligerence of the young. Frequently we saw them pushing and shoving each other, and once one dangled briefly by one foot, hanging over the edge of the nest. Three of the four young survived the thirty-five-foot fall, including the youngest and smallest, but one of the larger owlets disappeared. Since we weren't there at the time, we can only guess what happened. Höglund and Lansgren have suggested that young Great Grays leave the nest before they are fully fledged, voluntarily leaping down from even tall nest sites, in order to escape from the heat of the sun shining on the open nest. Observers at other nests have noted that owlets when two weeks old may walk out onto adjacent branches, returning to the nest and the warmth of the female for the night.

Wahlstedt, studying a nest in northern Sweden, reported that the female was never seen in the nest except during a hot day or a heavy rain when she returned to the nest to shelter the young. Otherwise, she watched the nest and young from a nearby tree, while the male fed the young directly. The food supply was good and sometimes the young were overfed. "On several occasions it was observed that those young which climbed out on the branches of the nest tree became so satiated that they fell into a deep sleep. They lay on their stomachs, crosswise on the branch, with head and tail hanging helplessly down toward the ground. They very much resembled seasick people hanging over the railing of a boat. At times they took so careless a position I was much afraid they would fall down to the ground while asleep" [translation].

On our first visit after the nest fell, we found the young birds on the ground and on low perches near the nest tree, but within a few days they were able to climb up into trees. Like parrots, these downy owlets hitched themselves upward with their strong feet, hooking their bill or biting into the bark for purchase, or reaching over a branch for a higher grip. Their short, poorly feathered wings served to balance them as they slowly progressed upward. They climbed most effectively on slanted trunks, but they were able to go up straight trunks if there were enough close branches. Over the next two weeks, though they were unable to fly, we would find them as high as twenty feet in spruce and tamarack trees, increasingly farther from the nest tree. According to Thomas C. Dunstan and Steve D. Sample, young Barred Owls climbed in trees to heights of up to forty-seven feet.

Pellets, regurgitated lumps of indigestible material, are cast up by all raptors. Feathers, claws, fur, and bones, whatever isn't digested is neatly compacted in the stomach and ejected from the mouth. Great Gray Owl pellets, up to three inches long and about an inch in diameter, were often found and collected. Analysis of their contents later identified the prey being taken. As expected, based on what we had seen the male bring to the nest, meadow and red-backed voles were most common. When the young owls were small and eating mainly flesh, they cast no pellets, but later, when they ate whole voles, their small pellets were ingested by the female, which helped to keep the nest clean. Few pellets were found beneath the nest, but a heap of pellets was found beside a low stump by a pool where the female evidently bathed. Some of these pellets contained chalky excrement, evidence that the female had also eaten the young owls' feces. At later stages, the owlets forcibly ejected feces over the edge of the nest.

We rarely saw owls cough up pellets, but one day, watching an owlet that had left the nest, I had a good view of the proceedings. One of the larger young, stand-

A moment of rest at midday for a female and the large nestlings.

ing upright on a branch, with neck extended upward, gave a few, quick, jerking movements that presaged the arrival of the pellet from the stomach. Gaping widely as the pellet appeared in its mouth, the youngster, instead of dropping it, held it in its bill for a minute or two—as if it didn't quite know what it had and was unsure whether to drop it or swallow it—before letting it fall. I retrieved the pellet and found it was coated with a thin layer of mucous, a slick, membranous envelope that obviously made it easier to regurgitate. The shiny coating dried rapidly, but long afterward was still discernible. The pellet, like most, was blunt on the lower end and slightly tapered on the upper, taking the shape of the proventriculus where it had been formed.

With the young out of the nest, the male delivered food directly to the two older young, and they responded to his appearance by giving loud begging cries. He continued to do all the hunting, the female remaining near the young. When the young showed signs of distress upon being handled by us, the female often perched nearby. Once, she perched so close I captured her by simply reaching out and seizing her feet. Banded and released a few minutes later, she dropped to the ground, turned around and glared at us, ruffled her plumage, and then flew away. Five minutes later she was back on the same perch close beside me, watching closely while the young were being banded.

A few times the female took dead prey off the end of a branch held out before her. The first time, she seized a vole with her bill, flew off about a hundred feet to another perch, chewed on the vole, tore it apart by holding it under one foot, then dropped it. Half an hour later when she was perched about eight feet above me, I offered another vole to her in the same way. This time she plucked it off and soon gulped it down. I tried this again a week later, first holding a vole carcass on a stick in front of the female, then, when she failed to respond, walking over and offering it to one of the older young. Incredibly, the female came winging in from about fifty feet away and, without pausing in flight, flew over the owlet and snatched the vole off the stick. She landed nearby on a higher perch, shredded the vole, and then carried off a portion, which she fed to the youngest owl, the latter having remained in her particular charge. She then returned and ate the remains she had left on the perch.

Long afterward I discovered that this was not the first time someone had fed a mouse to an owl in this manner. Napier Smith, encouraged by an old woodsman one day in May 1915, enjoyed a similar experience with a nesting male Hawk Owl near Ottawa. When a freshly killed "field mouse" on the end of a stick was held out to the bird, which was perched on a twelve-foot stump, the owl "stopped squealing and cocked his head from one side to the other, giving him such a droll appearance that I laughed aloud. On my advancing the mouse to the top of the stump, almost touching him, he opened his beak and gave a slight squeal; for a moment his pupils contracted, the yellow irises appearing enlarged, then, like a flash, he snatched the mouse from the stick with his claw. The next moment he was off with the mouse as buoyant as a feather, squealing as he flew through the woods."

A few minutes after the female took the dead vole off my stick, the male, who had been feeding the two older young, flew in with a vole in his bill, landing on a long, slanted pole several feet below an owlet perched near the end. The male walked up the limb toward the young, placing one foot before the other, wings upright for balance. Just as he reached the owlet, the female flew in from some distance, landed on the tip of the pole, causing it to sway, reached over the young owl's head and snatched the vole from the male's bill! At once she turned and flew off, carrying the vole over to feed to her young charge. It all took place in a few seconds and was a beautiful sequence to see as well as a further example of parental solicitude. Except for her special care, the young owl might have perished. Still, our observations agree with those of Höglund and Lansgren, who note that "it is probably a general rule that those young which get left behind in development will succumb sooner or later."

The sight of a dead vole evidently is a strong stimulus to a hungry owl. At one nest, we had placed three fledglings on a low limb to attract the female. As usual, the young owls were aggressive toward each other and to us. To test their feeding response, I held a dead vole by the nape in my lips and approached one of the larger, bill-snapping owlets. It immediately focused its attention on the vole, and, when I leaned close, tipped its head slightly to one side, then took it from me and gulped it down. I tried this at another time with an undernourished but grown young owl found in Winnipeg in November. Within a few days this bird gave begging calls whenever I entered the room in which she was kept to feed her. On three occasions she took mice from my mouth, always first gently nibbling on the mouse, then taking a firm hold and pulling until I let go.

The close relationship we felt with the nesting female changed abruptly the day her level of tolerance was breached. While I was trying to replace a struggling owlet on a branch above my head, the female suddenly attacked me, knocking off my cap and glasses, and sending me to my knees. Though frightened by the unexpected blow, I suffered only a minor scratch on my cheek. Later, when I was carrying the young owl to another location, the female slammed into the back of my head and neck, knocking me flat on my face. It was a shockingly strong blow to come from such a light, heavily feathered bird.

At Bob Taylor's insistence, I caused the female to attack three more times, holding a young owl while it flapped its wings and snapped its bill. The first time, the female came in so fast I threw myself down on one elbow to avoid her, and it appeared she had tried to strike the young. To ward off the female at the last moment, in order to protect both the young and myself, I then held a branch in one hand. Again she attacked, diving fast and low, and this time she struck the branch with one wing. We soon stopped photographing the diving owl, for it was clear that one of the three of us could get hurt.

At the nest, in our experience, the female is the aggressor. Moreover, her aggressiveness toward us seemed to be a response to distress signals from the young, rather than identification of humans as potential enemies. We were seldom attacked unless we were harassing the young. Since the female alone incubates the eggs and broods the young, her attachment to the nest is stronger than that of the male.

The tolerance so often shown by the female may be mainly an indication of her strong bond to the clutch or brood. Sometimes a female on a nest may even permit herself to be touched or pushed by hand. Similar strong broodiness is found in a variety of birds, e.g., bitterns, rails, falcons, and bluebirds. With continued visits to a nest, the incubating owl may show increased tolerance. But as the owlets increase in age, the female may show signs of agitation during nest visits. One learns to watch her behavior closely to reduce the amount of disturbance and to avoid being attacked. Her posture, facial expression, and vocalizations all provide signs of varying degrees of annoyance. When her wings are held out loosely and downward, when her bill is fully exposed, when she is standing upright, then it is time to be careful. Individual owls vary in behavior, but it pays to be wary. An owl that has permitted an observer to raise her off eggs one day, may later unexpectedly launch an aggressive attack. Brooding owls can be dangerous.

Höglund and Lansgren reported of Great Gray Owls in Sweden: "As a general rule the female was the most savage and defended nest and young many a time so frantically that it was difficult to make a close examination of the nest. In most cases it was necessary to use a mask for the face to protect from serious injuries. . . ." Wahlstedt, observing at a nest in Sweden, reported that on one occasion a male came flying in with a vole for the young while the female closely watched two observers beneath the nest tree. The male took no notice of the observers and flew directly to the female to give her the prey. The female became very irritated at this and buffeted the male so hard with her head that he lost his balance and had to take flight, in the process dropping the vole.

The male occasionally tried to lure us away, especially when the female uttered strong distress calls. He was usually relatively quiet and unobtrusive, and we had to look for him some distance from the nest. When approached, the watching male turned and flew off low and heavily, sailing just above the shrubs or suddenly dropping low, almost to the ground, an attractive ruse that impelled one to hurry after him. When we caught up with him we found him sitting on a perch, looking back over his shoulder and watching us. When we got closer, he fled again, but it was a conspicuous flight, and there was little doubt that this was distraction display, behavior serving to lead us away from the nest.

Our close contact with the adults was lost once the young could fly. Each time we found the young birds deeper in the woods, and when we approached them they flew away. We saw the three young for the last time at the end of July, locating them by listening for their loud calls. In addition to giving the food-begging call,

they occasionally gave a double-noted barking sound. They were fairly noisy, and called repeatedly, especially when a parent bird flew by, but they also responded to each other. On one occasion they flew from point to point until the oldest two were only ten feet apart and about forty feet from the youngest. Though out of the nest for seven weeks, they were staying together. By this time their wings and tails were fully feathered, but they still had downy heads and necks. I found one youngster being harassed by several birds, a mob scene involving a Common Flicker, Blue Jay, Gray Jay, and several Black-capped Chickadees. The owl flew off clumsily when I approached, flapping away with legs dangling, and made an awkward landing on a branch.

So we left them, apparently being fed by one or both parents, still not more than an eighth of a mile from the nest tree, but well hidden in a deep stand of tamarack. Their survival seemed assured, and we were not surprised to hear that a group of three Great Gray Owls, presumably this brood, had been seen in the general vicinity as late as September.

The length of time the young are dependent upon the parents for food is uncertain. I think they may be fed for three months or longer after leaving the nest, and social ties may endure even after the young have begun to forage for themselves. Two Great Gray Owls were seen in midmorning on October 1, 1978, in a heavily forested area in west-central Manitoba; they were heard hooting for half an hour before they were sighted. One bird, flushed from the ground, landed in a tree and hooted, whereupon the second owl flew in and perched above it. The latter hooted about six times, then both birds flew away. Parent and offspring? Nestmates? Whatever the case, two or more Great Gray Owls sometimes seen in close association in winter may be evidence of a continuing family bond.

11

In Search of Nests

There is a time between winter and spring which, for a searcher of owl nests, is ideal for roaming through woods and bogs. It varies in length with each season, but is never long enough. It is that time when the snow has almost disappeared, when insects are scarce, and when it is possible to see far ahead through the leafless trees.

Then the first pale green aspen leaves begin to flicker, and in a week this fresh color is spread across the tops of trees. Though we rejoice in the addition of color to the landscape, the growing leaves restrict our vision.

For many days after the aspens have leafed out, however, we can still see through the leafless tamaracks. But one warm day the first needles appear, emerging in tufts from tiny gray nubbins on each twig, and overnight there is a new fullness. At first merely a haze, a pale brush of green, the tamaracks quickly thicken with new growth, even though the needles may be less than a quarter-inch in length. Once the soft, feathery needles have fully emerged, the search for nests in tamarack bogs is a slow process. The hope of finding another nest, however, is strong incentive, and we have plodded through bogs in June and even into July.

In summer the bog is many shades of green, different tones in sun and shadow. The carpet of mounded, soft sphagnum moss, the leaves and stems of a multitude of other plants, all are green, and all reach out lovingly for the sunlight that streams down through the trees. In the humid heat the bog is like a greenhouse, and the liquid calls of Connecticut Warblers and Ovenbirds add to a growing sense of being in some tropical region. The feeling is enhanced by the sight of a colony, a grove of showy lady's-slippers. Like gaily colored feathered wands from a carnival thrust into the sphagnum mat, these waist-high, exotic plants rise from papery, pale green, furled leaves. They stand at the peak of flowering, startling white and pink voluptuous blossoms poised in the filtered light of this lacy, green retreat.

The edges of open bogs, rich with sedges and grasses, provide good habitat for meadow voles.

The two years following the much-studied Minnesota nesting were disappointing in that, despite intensive searching, we were unable to find an active nest. In 1973, however, we found a nest with a single, half-grown owlet. Encouraged, we searched even harder the following year, and managed to find three nesting birds in early stages of egg-laying and incubation. In 1975 we failed to find an active nest, but in 1976 we had four nests under close observation. Since two of these were in Minnesota and two were seventy-five miles northwest of Winnipeg, we were kept busy. In the next three years we had eight, two, and ten nests, respectively, for a total of twenty, all in Manitoba. We suspect that birds nested in Minnesota in 1979, but we simply ran out of time to check. Accounts of the discovery of nests from 1973 to 1976, and subsequent events, provide the main basis for this chapter. A final portion covers some unexpected activities at three 1977 nests.

In mid-June 1973 a report of a Great Gray Owl seen carrying prey led Robert Taylor and me to search for a nest in a bog about fifty miles east of Winnipeg. Relying on this one brief observation as certain evidence of a nearby nest, Bob and I spent most of a warm afternoon looking in this wet and tangled spruce-tamarack bog. We clambered over deadfalls in spruce stands, splashed through open areas of sedge, and looked carefully in two small islands of mature aspen, searching every tree for a nest, and listening for sounds of hungry young owls. It was soggy underfoot and sweltering; we constantly brushed away blackflies, mosquitoes, and sweat, meanwhile pushing onward, moving slowly from one grove to another, looking in every habitat type. Caught up in the excitement of the chase, we persistently searched, occasionally stopping to rest and briefly examine some bright bog flower.

Three hours later, when Taylor called to me from some distance, I had had enough excitement and beauty. I finally found him in a grove of small tamarack, leaning against a tree and looking exhausted. I sank down upon the nearest trunk and tiredly asked where we should search next. Grinning, he motioned upward. I leaned back and was surprised to find myself looking at an owlet standing on a nest, not fifteen feet above us. The nest had been found! Hastily, I wiped my steamy glasses, sweating face and eyes, then feasted upon the spectacle of the nestling peering fixedly down at us. "How did you find it?," I asked. "Just walked right up to it," was Taylor's simple reply. While we rested, we looked and listened for the adult birds, but not until I began to climb the tree to check on the nest contents did they appear, and then they were in sight only briefly. So dense was the tree growth in the vicinity of the nest tree that we couldn't see them unless they were perched close to the nest, but we could hear them hooting in alarm at our intrusion.

We blazed a quarter-mile trail back to the road and found ourselves about a half-mile from where we had begun our search—tired, wet, and thoroughly pleased with our success. Later, companions who visited this nest with us expressed surprise at the locality. From the road, the stunted tamarack seemed unsuitable habitat for Great Gray Owls. Even the nest, which was small and in a tangle of branches on a deformed tamarack, was unlikely looking. There wasn't much room for the adults to get in and out of the nest; later, we saw both male and female swoop in over the tops of the trees, and gained a new appreciation for their dexterity in flight.

The following year as well, this nest was again occupied. On a visit in late May, Spencer Sealy and I saw the female sitting low and tight to the nest, but she suddenly departed as we neared the tree. When she left the nest, a small, downy chick fell out, to our horror landing in a

pool of water below. We hurriedly dried it off with a handkerchief and placed it in the nest beside an even younger chick and an unhatched egg. Quickly backing away, we soon were relieved to see the female return. She walked along a branch to reach the nest, peered into it, lowering and weaving her head from side to side as she scanned the contents, then carefully settled onto the nest.

Newly hatched chicks, snuggled up under the female's feathers or between her feet, can accidentally be carried out of the nest if the female makes an abrupt departure. This unnerving experience taught us that there is potential risk in visiting an active nest during early stages. Although Henderson reported that a female Great Gray Owl returned and sat on an empty nest a few minutes after he had collected the full clutch of eggs, we later had a bird desert after it had laid four eggs.

Ideally, nests should be observed infrequently and from a distance, though this limits what can be learned. When I fret about the effects of our studies on Great Gray Owls, however, I am consoled by the thought that while we are disturbing factors at a few nests, there must be many other owls nesting in unknown sites, completely undisturbed by man.

On a return visit a few days later to the nest mentioned above, Sealy, wary of the possibility of a similar incident, crept forward and beneath the nest before the female flushed. Again, when she left the nest a chick went out with her. With a quick lunge, Sealy managed to catch the chick in mid-air, but not before it had struck a small twig. Though we didn't realize it at the time, this bird, the last to hatch, was seriously injured, for on the next day we found it lying dead on the ground beneath the nest. The female was still in attendance, however, and the other two young were in good condition. Ten days later, we were dismayed to find that the skimpy nest had collapsed, and there was no sign of adults or young. Thereafter, we tried to keep nests in good repair, using wire screen to give them additional support if necessary.

At the third nest studied that year, two of three young successfully fledged. In many respects this nest was the most pleasant to visit and the easiest to observe. But it was so close to civilization we were always uneasy. Adjacent to farmland and not far from a road, the nest was reached by a short walk through an open aspen woods and over a granite outcrop where a few large jack pine grew. An old, compact nest about twenty feet above ground in the forks of a mature trembling aspen was the site chosen by this pair of owls. It was a site we had visited as early as February, for owls had been present here and in nearby farm fields throughout the winter.

Before the eggs had hatched, Bob Taylor erected a light, metal tower about four feet from the nest tree. When I climbed the tower in late May, the female flew off the nest when I was halfway up, aggressively snapping her bill and hooting while in flight. A newly hatched chick, barely able to hold up its head, and two eggs, one just beginning to hatch, were in the nest. A minute later, the female returned, flying in aggressively, landing hard on the nest and accidentally striking the chick with one of her talons. Although the blow knocked the chick over, it survived, but I felt guilty. Two days later, when two young were present and the third egg was well pipped, Taylor climbed the tower, photographed the female, who remained on the nest, then put out his hand and touched her to force her off the nest. (At another of our nests, studied intensively by graduate student Michael Collins, the female became so used to his presence she would permit him to touch her, and often she stayed on the edge of the nest while the nestlings were weighed on a balance scale set in the nest.)

We spent many relaxed hours at this nest, for these were elegant surroundings: moss and lichen-covered rocks, greening woods, and a clear view of the nest from where we sat on a grassy bank about thirty yards from the nest tree. On a warm day in late May with wildflowers in bloom and birds in full song, this was an ideal situation. From one sun-warmed spot we could see anemones, violets, strawberries, blueberries, and saskatoons in full flower. Meanwhile, there was time to sort out the bird calls: Ovenbird, White-throated Sparrow, Swainson's Thrush, Blue Jay, Least Flycatcher, and Rose-breasted Grosbeak, a surprising assortment against which to listen for the soft hooting as the pair of owls kept in touch with each other. This was quite different from the tamarack bog sites of other nests where Myrtle and Connecticut warblers, Winter Wrens, and Gray Jays had kept us company.

In late June and July, long after leaves had obscured our view of the nest, a major infestation of forest tent caterpillars had an astonishing effect. The nest tree and surrounding aspens and shrubs of all kinds were denuded of leaves by hungry caterpillars, opening up the canopy and letting in light as in spring. At the height of the infestation, everything in sight was covered with the dark, striped caterpillars, a crawling mass that moved in all directions, even flowing across the nest and between the downy young. The droppings from thousands of caterpillars pattered on the forest floor like rain. The owls seemed to pay no attention to the hordes of caterpillars, the male bringing voles and the female feeding them to her offspring as usual.

Now, as the male was no longer concealed by foliage, we often saw him sitting in sight of the nest, but at some distance. Usually he sat for long periods with closed eyes, relaxed and silent, but he was attentive to sounds at the nest. Whenever we disturbed the female, he at once became alert and peered toward the nest. But, like other males we had observed, he never showed the aggressiveness of the female. At midday on bright days he often sought shade in which to rest.

The young grew rapidly, and by the end

of June were out of the nest and about a hundred yards away, perched on low branches and being carefully watched by the female. Late one evening we brought the young back to the vicinity of the nest tree The next morning we were at the site at 4:30 a.m., in time to see them being led off. The female lured the young chiefly by perching a little distance away and about five feet off the ground, repeatedly giving a muted *"wowk!"* or *"whoop!"* Upon hearing this call, the young scrambled along the forest floor, through a heavy growth of sedge, over fallen limbs and up on slanted trees. They climbed rapidly and capably, balancing with their small wings, and hopping "hand over hand" as they went upward. Though still less than a month old, they could leap across a space of two feet from one perch to another.

The male's hunting grounds were mainly the same open farmlands used during the winter. The female, trapped and color-marked by us, was a familiar bird. Both male and female had fed regularly on meadow voles taken through the snow. Now, in early summer, these same uncut alfalfa fields and grassy ditches still held considerable numbers of voles, and here occasionally we observed the male

hunting. On June 2, arriving at 4:55 a.m., we found the male already busy hunting, perched on a telephone pole beside the road. While Sealy went in to watch at the nest, I had the male constantly in sight until 6:12 a.m., when he flew off to the nest with a vole. During this entire period he hunted actively, flying from pole to pole, gliding over a field, dropping down and standing on the ground, peering about, hopping along, and several times pouncing unsuccessfully. Once he passed by me within forty feet in a slow glide, wings slanted upward like a giant Harrier, and again—while I stood motionless—he sailed past within ten feet!

The male's hunting urge on this morning seemed intense, as if nest, young, and mate, some combination of stimuli kept him compulsively trying to capture prey. At 6:00 a.m. he went down in a long glide onto the far end of the open field, stood nearly motionless for ten minutes while peering intently, then rapidly hopped about, making short pounces, jumping up with wings partly raised and striking hard at the ground. Then, having captured prey, he crouched over like a cat feeding, head down and back curved; twice he lowered his face to his feet. He stayed for a long time in this position, seeming in no hurry, and apparently enjoying his catch. This surprised me since he had seemed anxious to get food for the family. When finally he raised his head there was a vole in his bill. After a few seconds he flew off into the woods, arriving shortly thereafter at the nest where Sealy saw him give the vole to the female.

Another day, I found the male perched on top of a telephone pole in the same area at 4:30 a.m. Again, obviously busy hunting, he paid little attention to my presence. To my disappointment, for I had hoped to capture and band him, he showed little interest in a live white mouse that I let run about on the road directly beneath him.

Watching this great bird in bright daylight perched above me and flying slowly past, almost as if I didn't exist, was enthralling. I worried, however, thinking how small its chances of survival were. Absurdly bold, frightfully conspicuous; a ready victim of the automobile, an easy target for gunners. That this particular owl and his mate and family survived, as they did, was a matter of good luck.

Not all of our efforts to find nests were successful. On numerous occasions we vainly searched areas where there was evidence that birds were nesting. One day in June my sons and I saw a Great Gray Owl with a vole in its bill fly out of a roadside ditch and off across a heavy stand of spruce. More than ten man-days were spent searching in that area for an active nest. We finally concluded that the nest or young to which the bird had been flying must have been farther back in the woods than we were able to search. We did find, however, a large nest forty feet up in an aspen, apparently occupied by Broad-winged Hawks that circled and called overhead. I returned to the site a week later, driven by a hunch, and used tree-climbing spurs to check the nest. It was hot and humid and the air was thick with mosquitoes. In a way, although it

was a difficult climb, it was good to get above the ground. Although no Broad-wings were present, the nest had been lined in their fashion with fresh twigs and strips of old bark. Beneath the new lining I discovered old Great Gray Owl feathers, an indication that this nest may have been used by them in the previous year! With that in mind, we checked the nest each year, and in the spring of the third year were gratified to find it occupied by Great Gray Owls.

For several weekends in late spring 1976, Herb Copland and I heard Great Gray Owls calling at night from deep in a tamarack bog in northern Minnesota. One night my first attempt to start the owls calling elicited a clear chorus of wolves! Each time I hooted, the wolves shattered the night with their loud howling. When I tried to imitate the wolves, however, they remained silent. But almost every night we heard owls, and once one flew by almost overhead. Each day we searched in vain for a nest; it was tantalizing.

In mid-May we were encouraged by an especially long bout of calling. We listened to the low hooting, trying to fix in our minds the location of the calling bird. It had been dark when we began, but now, from a heavy cloud layer that merged with the darker forest came the moon— first a pale orange light along the edge of the cloud, then a warm red orb rising into the sky, and finally the round full moon, brilliant pearly gray. Standing on the roadside in the bright light, amused to see our shadows so clearly, we debated venturing into the woods in hopes of finding the bird. Reason prevailed (knowledge of the many deadfalls, interminable thickets, unseen dangers of dead limbs), sending us away some time after midnight.

Determined to find a nest, we returned the following weekend. What happened on that occasion may perhaps best be conveyed in the following excerpt from a letter I dashed off to a close friend shortly after returning to Winnipeg:

A fledgling sits on a log close to the forest floor. At four to five weeks of age, the flight feathers are well under way.

"Arrived home today, May 30, 4:30 p.m. after gruelling weekend, but happiness galore, result of finding another active (migawd) Great Gray Owl nest today. Persistent belief in analysis of observations during previous weekends (noctural seance, calls drifting back and forth from me to owl and vice versa) as full moon arose. Convinced that owls were on territory, Herb and I drove down there on Saturday afternoon, went into bog at 8:30 p.m. An hour later found male owl hunting; it came and snapped its bill and hooted at us—pure aggressive display on territory I said, and we hung about in woods until 10:30 p.m. forgodsakes—and I saw two beaver on dammed drainage ditch, slipped in and got wet but didn't care, it was so great for the owl to have come out and approached and snapped at me (as if I mattered!)

Went to bed late and arose early and sashayed back into the bog at dawn in the mist and heavy, heavy dew (especially on the equisetum, that stuff is made for dew, until one is soaked to the waist almost) and found the male hunting again in another mature tamarack stand, and this time we stood ever so long and finally saw it fly off with mouse in bill (which is sure indication of nest nearby) and trudged off and wandered about, with control man on point on cutline, and first I found two old empty nests, then another, and exhausted, sent Herb off on another round, while I stood and watched for the male. Herb about twenty minutes later gave a great shout and I responded in kind and then we met in woods and he had found the nest! and we went back and gawd there she was this gorgeous female with huge head and snapping bill while I climbed the tree first time ever, about twenty-five feet, branches breaking and almost fell but I have become a squirrel and clung and made it up and lo and behold an egg, another egg pipping, and a tiny chick! And down again, and away and watched her come back on the nest and

then back-tracked a mile and a half through the tamaracks, few insects, but still hot and moist and lovely and a Mourning Warbler nest and a Song Sparrow nest, and mostly great clusters of pitcher plants and lady's-slippers and sphagnum and wet to the waist again and gawd how I loved it all. So a fifth nest for Minnesota and no one else knows where this faraway nest is and it is a great spot remote and most beautiful and we will check it again in three weeks or so and band the young and how you would love it!"

Three weeks later we found three young in the nest, attended by the alarmed female. While we lowered the young from the nest for banding, she remained perched on the tops of the highest trees in the vicinity. On our two later trips to the nest site, made in an effort to capture the female, she remained elusive. Even when we held the struggling young birds out for her to see, though much upset, she failed to come close enough for us to snare. She was by far the shyest female we had yet encountered at a nest.

Far less aggressive than any other female owl in our experience, she showed strong distraction display, especially when we brought a dog in to the site. This was an extra effort on our part to lure her within reach. We gathered the three young, which at this later date we found perched in trees within a few hundred feet of the nest tree, and placed them in a row on a low, horizontal limb. Then I urged my springer spaniel to bark, growl, and leap up toward the bill-snapping owlets. This created a considerable row and elicited a tumultuous display by the female. Uttering screams like a Red-tailed Hawk, mewing sounds, mournful hoots, and startling, heronlike squawks, the female flew down near us, flinging herself with widespread wings against low branches, seemingly in utter abandon. This display set the dog charging after her, drawn to the sight and sound of a bird floundering and flapping in low boughs. We were frightened, for at times it looked as if she could break her flight feathers, so violently did she thrash about. A moment later, as the dog ran toward her, she was upright and watchful, looking back at it. Then she flew off slowly, close to the ground, keeping ahead of the dog, before swooping up toward another perch. Each time she went through the same motions. When the dog was called off, the owl soon returned to a high perch as before, hooting softly, looking out across the forest and down at her offspring. When the dog was sent out again, the shrieking female dived down through the trees in a pell-mell, headlong plunge, flinging herself against boughs with flapping wings, repeating her display.

No matter how many times we tried, we couldn't get close to this bird. Despite her apparent abandon, whenever I approached with the snare-pole, she moved away or returned only to perch high above us. We couldn't think of anything else we could do to lure her within reach, and finally gave up.

I returned to the site again in early July, determined to make a final effort to capture the female. As my friends and I approached the site, we heard the female owl calling, and a few minutes later we found one of the owlets perched upright on top of a tall stump right beside the trail. The female circled above us on widespread wings, calling vigorously in alarm, while we searched for other young. In a few minutes I found a second owlet about fifteen feet high in a tree. I brought it down and carried it to a clearing, making it snap its bill and flap its wings in an effort to attract the female. She was much more agitated than she had been on previous visits and to my elation she suddenly landed on the top of a broken tree within range of my snare-pole. I quickly set the owlet down, reached for the pole and found that the snare wire was caught on a tiny twig. . . . I couldn't free it! And still the female sat and watched. In des-

peration, I wrenched the snare loose and although the wire loop was hanging crookedly, reached as high as I could and managed with considerable effort and shaking hands to bring the snare down over her head. Then I pulled her off the perch, bringing her flapping to the ground where I at once pounced upon the struggling bird, finally seizing her strong legs in my bare hands. In an outrageous feeling of triumph I raised her high and shouted aloud with joy and relief. I had her now and wasn't about to lose her. So, with the help of my friends (Karen Eastman and Charles Newell), we soon had her measured, banded, and marked. All the while, she just lay back in my arms, strong feet and sharp talons safely held out of the way with my two hands, blinking her wide eyes and occasionally giving deep glances at the owlet perched nearby. When finally I turned her loose, she landed not far off, great ruffled wings sagging, panting, a little overheated, but in a few minutes she was back to normal, perched high in the top of a tree, still keeping an eye on her offspring.

After gathering up our gear, we slowly made our way back through the tamaracks, taking more time now to admire various bog flowers and plants—orchids of several kinds, pitcher plants—and stopping to identify with delight a tiny nest with eggs of the Lincoln's Sparrow, a bird whose song we had heard on the way to the nest site. Our day was further brightened by the light, lilting song of a Winter Wren coming from a distant grove.

The following year, when we had eight active nests under observation, we found further evidence of the variable behavior shown by female owls. Some were wary and completely unapproachable, but one came right down to our level when we began to band her young; she was taken readily and gently with the snare-pole. We were able to bring her to the ground, slip the barely tightened noose off, band and mark her in a relatively short time and

A magical moment—the male delivering food to the female at a nest high above the ground. Both owls close their eyes briefly when the female takes the prey from his bill.

The male glides away from the nest after the female has taken the prey. He may doze on a nearby branch until a call from the female causes him to begin hunting again.

with a minimum amount of handling. A few minutes later she perched near us, colored wing tag conspicuous against her plumage, watching intently while we finished banding the young. When we left the site, it was as if she had never been handled by us; she flew up high to perch and call, giving weird distraction sounds, before eventually slipping out of our sight when we were some distance from the nest site.

At another nest, a female we had come to know as a fairly docile bird unexpectedly attacked me when I climbed the nest tree to bring down the young. Twice she struck me on the back of the head, giving me plenty of warning that her mood had changed. I pulled my cap down tighter, then, clinging with one arm to the trunk of the tree, tried to bundle one of the nestlings into a sack. At that moment the female flew directly toward me, coming fast across the nest with both feet held out before her, reaching toward my face with talons spread wide. I reacted without thinking, grabbing one of her feet in my gloved hand, then spent a few confusing minutes trying to bring her under control without hurting her or myself. I hung on to that one foot while she flapped her wings and struggled for balance, meanwhile clawing me with her free foot in the belly and on one thigh. It was a perilous moment, for I still had to hang onto the tree with one arm, but I was not ready to lose my hold on the bird. Meanwhile, my companion on the ground could only watch with alarm, repeatedly asking if I was all right. I soon had the poor bird tucked under my arm and was eventually able to grasp both her feet. After resting briefly I happily tucked her headfirst into the sack and brought her down for banding.

A few weeks later, visiting another nest to band the last young of the season, I again captured a bird by hand, but with much less effort. Although this was a shy bird, one that always disappeared from the nest each time we approached, even when she was on eggs, she invariably came back as soon as we climbed to the nest. On several occasions she landed on the opposite side of the nest and, apparently tame and unaggressive, watched closely while I was there. This time I was hoping she would do the same thing, and I was ready for her, having secured a firm foothold at the level of the nest. In a moment she came winging back through the trees, straight to the nest; just before she landed I quickly grabbed both her feet, brought her flailing wings together, and tucked her under one arm. Before taking her down to be banded, I clung to my perch, looking into that impassive face, into those gleaming eyes, trying in vain to glimpse something of the spirit of the large bird, now captive, soon to be ignominiously shoved into a sack. It was with some sadness that I thought of the several other times she and I had exchanged glances, looking at each other across the small width of the nest, when she stood aloof, free and untouched, bound to the contents of the nest.

12

Nest Builders

In spring, wandering alone through a cool bog to check a nest, I am at peace. Though the busy world rattles on, I have, in an hour's drive, rid myself of aggressive, screeching traffic, dusty city streets, and personal cares. Early in the season before mosquitoes have hatched, my sojourn is free even of those distractions, and briefly I can lose myself in what I fancy is the owl's world. The snow has recently disappeared, but under the dry top of the sphagnum moss there is still ice, and the water that splashes up from low spots is cold. Pushing along the well-worn trail to the nest, boots sucking in and out of the bog, my passage is noisy and labored, probably more than that of the moose, whose sign I see before me. Pausing to catch my breath, my mind is filled with the moment: the sound of my breathing, a sharp "Whit!" from a hidden thrush, the brittle bark of a tamarack branch to which I cling for balance.

Because this nest was used last year, we have already checked it a dozen times this season, each time hoping it would hold an owl. So I approach the nest site cautiously and peer with binoculars from some distance, standing beneath the green boughs of a cedar. But there is no owl on the nest; there is only a shaggy mass of twigs on a crooked branch. But since I have come this far, I might as well look in the nest itself.

Climbing the tree to the nest is routine by now, and familiar branches and knots support fingers, knees, and toes. A quick glance shows an absence of eggs. But wait, where last week there had been merely a lining of weathered tamarack twiglets, there is now a feather! One fresh, fluffy Great Gray Owl feather. A bird has at least visited here, and I picture it flying up to the nest, landing hard and balancing on the edge, eyes glaring fiercely, then springing away, led onward by other demands, one lost feather left in the nest—a sign to bolster my hopes.

This photo shows the food exchange between a male and female at a nest deep in a tamarack swamp. Note the quill feathers on the nearest nestling.

The female closes her eyes as a nestling seizes the prey.

Owing to their habit of using stick nests built by other species, Great Gray Owls must have a natural propensity for searching out and visiting deserted or vacant nests. Scandinavian ornithologists have noted that to keep Great Grays nesting in an area it is important to repair existing nests. Not only do nests naturally deteriorate, but the species has a peculiar habit of scratching deep into nests when inspecting them, sometimes digging right through the bottom. Moreover, a season of use produces further wear. Imitation or man-made nests, reasonably close duplications of natural nests, have been used by several species of raptors. Twice, in Sweden, Great Gray Owls used man-made nests.

After the collapse in 1970 of a natural nest from which Great Gray Owls fledged, we decided to try to elicit further nesting by providing a substitute nest. In July, using a wire-mesh frame for a base, we built a nest of twigs in a deformed tamarack about fifteen feet above ground. This was several hundred yards from the original nest tree in a nearby tamarack woods where the owl family was residing. We were hopeful that the nest would be used the following spring by the parents or their offspring.

Our expectations increased when, in early March 1971, we found signs that a Great Gray had visited the nest. A thick, compact mass of snow often forms on top of nests at this time of year and it was evident that the owl had removed a considerable amount of snow by scratching and digging, presumably trying to get down to the nest. A single feather frozen to the snow remaining in the nest identified the visitor. Despite this early visit, however, the nest went unused that year, possibly because of a dearth of mice and voles in the vicinity. Still, it was good to know that owls had found the nest and were interested in it. Encouraged by this observation, we built more nests here and northward for about sixty miles, particu-larly where owls were seen in what we judged to be suitable nesting habitat.

Almost all our nests were built in tamarack trees, partly because nests in these deciduous conifers, we reasoned, must be more conspicuous from fall to spring than in other conifers, and because tamaracks are usually easy to climb. Where necessary, we drove in large spikes for climbing, or used climbing spurs, but in many cases we relied on branches alone. Nests were built at heights from ten to thirty feet. For a number of reasons, tamaracks are relatively easy trees in which to build nests. A tree with a deformed top makes a good nest support, especially where insect damage and disease have resulted in loss of the leader or tip of the tree, causing a growth of upright instead of horizontal branches. This ideal, basketlike arrangement makes the best support for a nest; simply cut out the dead tip, clear away a few branches, and the tree is ready to receive a nest. Similar sites, especially where the central limb has decayed, are often used by nest-building birds.

At first glance, a tree often has so many fine branches it is difficult to envision installing a nest. Sometimes it is necessary to climb the tree and make a closer inspection to ensure that there is adequate space for a nest. Once the decision is made, there ensues a vigorous trimming and alteration, clearing away unnecessary branches to open up the site. Large, dead branches, broken off the nest tree or from adjacent trees, are used to form a broad, thick base. Then smaller branches and twigs are added, tramped and packed down into a compact form about eighteen inches in diameter.

Much of this material has to be hauled up into the tree by rope, so the most effective operation calls for one person in the tree and another on the ground. In the final stage, fine sticks and twigs, crumbled by hand or broken and crunched underfoot, are added to form a dense lining.

Since Great Grays seem to prefer deep nests, I usually make a fair-sized depression in the center.

Where there were insufficient branches, a piece of wire screen was used as a base, and at times the sticks were wired onto the tree. Given a reasonably good nest site, it was sometimes possible to complete a nest in twenty minutes, but on at least one occasion it took two of us more than two hours to build one. A man-made nest doesn't usually look much different from a natural nest built by hawk or raven, but in choosing a nest site we also took into account the presence of nearby dead stubs for perches, and the nearness of old clearings and grassy places that would make good hunting grounds.

Finding a suitable tree usually took a lot longer than building the nest. Especially in winter, when many of our nests were built, we often spent hours driving about and hiking or skiing through woods, looking for the right tree. These winter excursions were enjoyable. Even at thirty below zero Fahrenheit it was pleasant exercise, at least on sunny days, though my teen-aged son, Woody, or Herb Copland, my usual companions, standing below in the snow and sending up tools and bundles or branches by rope, didn't always agree. Building nests in early spring or late fall, we finally decided, was much easier, though there were fewer weekends on which we could do this.

In the course of several seasons of building nests I gained a special fondness for the sturdy trunks and strong limbs of tamaracks, for their lichen-encrusted branches, friable twigs, and aromatic sap. Invariably, after a nest-building venture, I carried home some part of the tree—thin bark flakes, sticky twiglets, or tiny, round cones—on my clothing, in my pockets, or down my neck.

Although by January 1974 we had built thirty-five nests, none had been used by Great Grays. But we spent a lot of time each season checking nests, driving, walk-ing, climbing and, in some cases, just trying to find them. During this period, Red-tailed Hawks appropriated two of our nests, a Great Horned Owl used one as a platform on which to devour a snowshoe hare, and some predator finished off a red squirrel in another.

Reports in mid-April 1974 of Great Gray Owls in the general locality of our first man-made nest sent us to the area in a hurry. When we arrived at the nest site, we found the lining had been scratched out and twigs were scattered about on top of the snow. Several wet, bedraggled Great Gray Owl feathers were lying on the wire-screen bottom of the nest. I rebuilt the nest, adding branches to the edge and a new lining of fine twigs, carefully fitting them into position with silent, anxious hope.

Our next visit to the site was made on May 11. It was cold and raining lightly when we set forth across a clearing in the woods. Stumbling through the bog, both of us with misted glasses, Spencer Sealy and I stopped when still fifty yards from the nest tree. It was a wise move. Just barely visible through the dripping trees, the nest at first appeared to be empty. Great Gray Owls are usually conspicuous on a nest and we expected to see the owl's head protruding above it. We saw nothing; but, as we focused our binoculars, there was a movement, a wing lifted up, and then, to our delight, a Great Gray Owl slipped over the edge of the nest and away through the trees. She must have been lying flat in the nest.

We hastened forward, hardly daring to hope that there might be something in the nest. I scrambled up the trunk of the tree and was rewarded with the sight of two fresh white eggs, side by side. Shouting the good news to Spencer, I slid back down and we left right away so the female could get back on the nest. Considering how cold and wet it was, it seemed incredible that she had flown while we were still so far from the nest tree. Usually Great

Because Great Gray Owls have a habit of using vacant or deserted nests, rather than building them themselves, one way to keep the birds nesting in an area is for owl fanciers to repair existing nests or construct man-made ones. Here, the author hauls a bundle of branches up a tamarack tree during construction of a man-made nest in late winter.

A female Great Gray Owl sits on a man-made nest in a tamarack bog in early spring. The twisted branches that provided support for the nest may have resulted from past infestation by larch sawflies.

Grays sit tight to the nest, so we were afraid she might desert or the eggs get chilled. But, as we learned later, she came back, eventually both eggs hatched, and one youngster was successfully reared; the other disappeared. On a later visit, when we were able to observe the female more closely, we identified her as a bird that we had trapped, banded, and individually color-marked on March 30 within a quarter-mile of the nest tree. Thus, assuming it was the same bird that scratched out the lining of the nest in early March, this owl had been in the nest vicinity for at least two months.

This same nest, repaired and checked several times the following year, was found to have been visited by owls as early as mid-February. On April 1 we found a female on the nest, crouching low and watching us attentively as we approached. She stayed tight to the nest as we moved slowly forward, not flushing until we were within twenty-five feet of the tree. Although we were sure there would be an egg, there wasn't. There were several feathers, however, suggesting that she had been sitting on the nest for some time and that egg-laying was imminent. On our next visit, on April 3, we again found her on the nest, but this time we stayed far back, not wishing to disturb her during this critical period. From a vantage point several hundred yards away, we crouched amid small pools, sitting on damp mossy hummocks above the snow, but this soon proved uncomfortable. Finally, we arranged ourselves on an old tamarack log, breaking off the brittle, twisted branches so we could sit and watch in comfort. One time we saw her leave the nest, which was barely visible through the slender trunks and boughs, but she soon returned and settled down carefully, her manner suggesting she had at least one egg. Then she sank lower until only her head remained above the twigs that rimmed the nest. When I hooted softly, she swung her head about,

staring in our direction while we remained still, elbows on our knees, watching her every move through binoculars. Even at this distance we were wary of disturbing her, and remained motionless while she was looking toward us. Eventually we arose and departed in the cool evening, convinced that the bird was well established in our nest.

In time, four eggs were laid, but, shortly after incubation was underway, disaster struck. The parents were not to be found, and the four eggs were now only empty shells scattered on the ground, apparently eaten by Gray Jays. It was difficult to believe that the parents would have deserted the nest at this late stage. We guessed that either the male had been killed, forcing the female to desert, or else the female had been killed at the nest, either by a natural predator or by man. It was a great disappointment.

In mid-December 1975, inspired by the discovery of a few fresh Great Gray feathers hanging on twigs in fall and early winter in a tamarack woods close to a natural nest that had been occupied two years earlier, I invited a friend to help me build a new nest. This site was about fifty miles east of Winnipeg. It was a cold day when we set out, with about three feet of soft snow on the ground. Back in the bog it was dark and quiet, for it was a cloudy day. It was a new experience for my companion, who had not previously been in such habitat, and she was delighted to see dozens of White-winged Crossbills at close range feeding on tamarack cones. Cold hands and feet notwithstanding, she stood about in the snow while I searched for half an hour for a suitable tree. Then she patiently passed up to me the various materials I needed to build the nest. When the nest was finally completed, she insisted on climbing up to see the finished nest. With her soft mocassins, it was no easy feat to use the spikes I had driven into the frozen trunk. I was relieved when she had made her way safely back to the

A kind of third eyelid, the nictitating membrane sweeps across the eyeball from inner corner to outer, keeping the eye clean and moist.

This fledgling is still largely in down plumage, but its semi-circular facial disc pattern is already evident.

ground. Three hours had passed by the time we got back to the car.

The next time we visited this nest, in mid-May, it was warm, wet, and green in the bog. There were five downy young owlets in the nest, closely attended by a female. Built in mid-December, the nest had been occupied in early April, and here were the results! While we watched (my companion radiant at seeing her first Great Gray Owls), the male arrived with a vole, flew to the nest, gave it to the female, and disappeared over the tops of the trees.

My colleagues and I continued to build nests through the winter of 1975–76 and into spring, until we had more than fifty. In the fall and winter of 1976–77 we outdid ourselves. Ray Tuokko built an unprecedented thirty-six nests, often working by himself. I constructed another fourteen nests, relying on assistance from several people. This effort brought our total number of man-made nests to about a hundred. Of five nests that I installed in December along a three-mile stretch of road, three were occupied by Great Grays the following April. That season we had eight active nests, of which five were in man-made or reconstructed natural nests. In 1978 two of our man-made nests were used. In 1979, by which time we had built another thirty nests, we had ten active Great Gray Owl nestings. Of these, five were in man-made structures, and two were in rebuilt nests. To date, of thirty-two recent Great Gray Owl nestings, sixteen were in man-made nests, six in rebuilt nests, and ten in completely natural nests. In addition, our man-made structures were used by Great Horned Owls (twice), Long-eared Owls (twice), and Redtailed Hawks (five times). Porcupines used a few for winter roosts, raptors used a few for feeding platforms, and one was used as a summer roost by a bat, probably a hoary bat, judging by the size of the droppings. Some of our nests have been up for five and six years, but have never been visited by Great Gray Owls (or any other bird, so far as we can tell). These nests are well constructed and in apparently suitable locations, but evidently some feature is lacking. Although a few nests built in aspens in upland sites attracted owls, the best response has been obtained from nests built in spruce-tamarack or tamarack bogs, often over water. Since most of our nests are fairly durable, we expect to be checking them for many seasons.

Probably there are many natural nests available to Great Grays over much of their range. After all, it doesn't take a pair of Broad-winged Hawks long to build a new nest. In many areas of suitable habitat that we examined, however, there was a scarcity or absence of nests; partly on this account we have continued to build nests for owls. Man-made nests, in any case, provide additional nesting sites, and may lure owls from less accessible places. In some areas, where natural nests are scarce, man-made nests could be a useful management technique.

On a few occasions, nests built by us in March and April were visited by owls a few weeks later. The quickest occupancy of a nest occurred less than four weeks after it had been built (March 12, 1979). This suggests that the birds found this nest shortly after it was installed. By finding one or two fresh Great Gray Owl feathers, or even a downy feather fragment caught on a twig, we could tell that an owl had visited a nest. This meant that an owl had not only discovered the nest, not merely looked at it, but had spent some time in it, crouched down and scratching, testing, making some judgment that only owls perceive. Thus, even after the nesting season is underway, nonbreeding owls, or perhaps even a hunting male on his territory, quickly discover and visit new nests, possibly responding to an inner drive to catalog the location of nests well in advance of other seasons.

In our occupied Great Gray Owl nests we often find numerous tamarack twigs with the bark removed and the wood gnawed as if by a rodent. This is typical Great Gray Owl work. Protruding twigs that cause discomfort to the brooding female may be nibbled at over a long period in an attempt to remove them. In one nest, an owl's efforts to remove an offending twig evidently brought about the accidental trampling and loss of her eggs. However, in many successful nests small, loose twigs bear signs of nibbling, suggesting that owls find some satisfaction in this exercise. Perhaps it gives the female something to do during the long days on the nest. In some instances, the presence of a freshly nibbled twig is evidence, in the absence of a feather, that a Great Gray Owl has visited the nest.

Numerous visits are necessary to determine which nests are in use, to obtain egg-laying and hatching dates, and to band the young. Visiting a nest, however, provides more than an opportunity to gather information. Each visit is an adventure, exciting and sometimes offering unexpected delights. One early May day we were surprised to observe a male owl hunting in a small cattail marsh near a man-made nest in a spruce-tamarack bog.

When we neared the nest we walked with some apprehension because in April we had found the female on eggs, but we were aware that since our last visit she might have deserted. Upon our first, distant view of the nest, however, we could see the big, upright head of the brooding female. We moved forward, talking casually to reassure her, and she stayed on the nest, peering down at us with bright yellow eyes. Hesitating to disturb her, I tapped gently on the trunk of the tree, whereupon she flushed from the nest. Flying out over our heads, broad wings brushing against boughs, she flapped and then soared up to a high perch, meanwhile giving a soft alarm call and aggressively snapping her bill. I quickly climbed the tree, pulled myself up far enough to look over the edge of the nest, and found two white, downy young.

A few minutes after we withdrew, we saw the female return to the nest, land deftly on the edge, look down at the contents, then hop forward and shuffle about onto the owlets. When we saw that she was well settled, we headed out to the edge of the woods.

Hopes of finding a Sandhill Crane nest sent us into a nearby, nearly dry marshy bog, where in April we had seen a pair of cranes. The moment we walked out into the marsh, the strident clatter of crane voices rang out, and we saw the pair striding through the cattails and sedge a few hundred yards away. The female marched straight along, but the male circled about her, leaping up and flapping his wings. Close in front of us, at the same time, two loudly calling Common Snipe hovered with upright wings, circling over the vegetation. And two male Red-winged Black Birds, looking a little forlorn in the dry marsh, sang face to face.

And then, suddenly, we saw the *male* Great Gray Owl—upright and motionless, on a dead snag near the edge of the marsh, alert and actively hunting. It was the first time we had seen a Great Gray Owl in a marsh—the dark-plumaged bird contrasted strongly with the pale, dead grass and reeds. We slowly walked to within fifty feet of him, impressed by the rich brown and silvery-gray color of his plumage, vividly illuminated by the low evening light. From back in the woods the female owl called: a persistent, low, but penetrating single note. It seemed to stimulate the male. He moved from one black snag to another as if following a familiar route, peering intently from each perch. Finally, he dropped down out of sight; a moment later he came out carrying a vole in his bill. We followed his progress, lost him behind some willows, then saw him briefly as he headed into the trees toward the nest.

A few minutes later, while we were walking toward the cranes, the male owl reappeared, flew out to the same perch, and hunted intently once again, while his

mate continued to call. At this moment,
the cranes lifted and flew in tandem right
over the owl, calling constantly, their
loud calls echoing off the nearby trees so
fast it seemed as if two pairs were calling.
They flew off some distance, still calling
as they went down somewhere else, leaving us alone with the hunting owl.

We stood still, charmed by the sight of
the poised owl, reluctant to leave. As the
sun lowered, the light seemed to become
stronger, bringing everything into sharper
focus. The owl flew to a new perch, where
it was outlined against the pale sunset,
and strongly back-lighted. Now its colors
were indistinguishable; but light shone
through filmy portions of its plumage,
glowing brightly across the tip of the tail,
up one side of the body, and around the
margin of the head.

13

A Different Race of Creatures

On a day in early April, when edges of roads and woods are free of snow and dun-colored with last year's grass, I stoop to search for signs of mouse activity. Beneath clumps of old grass, I am pleased to find numerous damp runways and small, fresh, greenish droppings. The tops of newly arisen green leaves within the runways, freshly cropped by hungry voles, are further evidence. Nutrient-rich, succulent grass must be invigorating fare for animals that have survived the winter on dried stems and leaves. For early-nesting predators that depend on mice and voles for food, this activity has great importance.

I delight in the knowledge of all this fresh food out of sight beneath the matted grass, moving upward, drawn by the warm sun. I have visions of tiny, pink, blind mice clustered together in snug nests, nourished by sleek mothers fattened on this new vegetation. So I think: "Mice, grow! Reproduce—so that there will be plenty of food for owls yet to come." For not far away, in a cool, wooded grove where the snow lies more than a foot deep, I have seen a Great Gray Owl on a nest, covering her first egg.

A week later, the new grass leaves have pushed up through the old, and a light green color lies over all the dead grass. A faint buzzing of insects may be heard, and everywhere, the whistled calls of White-throated Sparrows. It is a busy time of year: willow catkins are emerging, leaves unfurling, the world is reaching out for sunlight, and in every thicket and hollow, birds are busily setting up territories, singing, and chasing with their special kind of madness.

Now the hen owl sits on three eggs, beside her a dead vole, excess food brought by her mate. Is he, I wonder, excited by the rustling and squeaking of mice and voles in shrubby meadows and grassy fields? Out of all the spring voices arising about him, the growing sounds of prey activity, their encounters, disputes, and hurrying feet, must be loud in his ears.

Focusing intently on prey, this owl is about to pounce.

It is not easy to write now that spring is here. At my desk, pen in hand, my mind wanders. I would rather be out in the still frozen bogs searching for yet another nest. We have looked in so many woods these past years it is bewildering to try to recall all the places where we have found or built nests. Each year is a new challenge. The sight of a nest, the shape of the tree that contains it, the surroundings—each situation is unique; and there have been more sites than I can easily recall. It is a group effort and between us, by quizzing and reminding each other of particular events, we manage to revisit almost every good nest each spring. Notebooks and maps help, but in the field there is a special delight as memory unfolds, as certain trees and landforms remind us of the direction to a nest.

Visiting known nests and searching for new nests each spring is a long, arduous task, and I often wonder where and when it will end. For how many more seasons will we do this? There are times when it seems senseless. And then, early one morning, after trekking a mile through the woods, following an old trail to a nest, led onward by broken saplings and faded colored marking tape, suddenly there is the nest, just as it was before. But wait, there is a new shape. Is that something on the nest? I fumble getting my binoculars into position, focus, and yes! The morning is ours, for a Great Gray Owl is there. And that is the incentive.

I still get pretty excited when I first see a Great Gray on a nest, and if it's one of our man-made nests, I can get fairly emotional. And why not? Owls can move over a lot of territory. A pair of owls moving into one of our nests is unusually satisfying. I feel like a surrogate parent—vain, jealous, protective, and should the nest fail, I am inordinately downhearted. But I ask myself the same question. How many more nests are we going to build? It's a long way to some of our artificial nests, driving and walking, and they need to be visited more than once during the season. We hardly have time now to check those we've already built. And yet, I keep thinking of special places, musing about certain sites in woods where I'm sure a nest would attract breeding owls. The urge to put up another nest is strong, to add one more nest to an empty forest, to try again to lure a pair of owls. Whatever the reason, science or pure enjoyment, I am likely to be there next April. The possibility of finding a nest occupied by a Great Gray Owl gives me all the excuse I need to wander in the bog.

There is no doubt that I have become charmed with tamarack bogs. The hours of fruitless stumbling and tripping over deadfalls, the swarms of blackflies and mosquitoes, the cold emptiness on some winter days—these are minor annoyances compared to the beauty of orchids and lush greenery, the songs of myriad birds, and the wonder of seeing Great Gray Owls at a nest site. Some readers may recall Aldo Leopold's story about the two Wisconsin farmers who, in their later years, took time to plant a truck-load of young tamaracks on their farm. After years of hard work, draining and clearing their land to survive, they realized they missed the wildflowers they used to enjoy, and so they struggled to replant a small tamarack bog. It is something I now can understand.

Today in Manitoba large tamarack-bog areas are being drained and cleared to obtain more agricultural land. Sometimes the peat is removed with bulldozers, but often it is burned off to expose the underlying mineral soil. In the best situations, where feasible, the peat is simply plowed into the underlying soil. But removal of peat by burning is still a widespread practice and peat smoke has become a highway traffic hazard. In many places, however, it is the peat that is sought. This resource is being dug up and shipped in plastic packages as far as the states of the Southwest for use as a natural mulch and fertilizer for gardens. So the organic debris accumulated during a thousand summers helps make flowers bloom in far-away deserts.

But peat has other values as well. The current energy shortage has given a new value to this substance. Next to coal, peat is America's second most abundant fossil fuel. It can be burned directly to produce power, and also can be converted into substitute natural gas. Half of the peat reserves of the United States are in Alaska, but the most readily accessible supply is in Minnesota, where there is an active program to develop peat for energy. Is peat mining likely to be a threat to Great Gray Owl habitat? (As I see it, some of the best habitat is in extreme southeastern Manitoba and northern Minnesota.) At the moment the answer is unknown, but replacement of peat is a slow process. In Minnesota, consideration is being given to the many values—including Sandhill Cranes, Great Gray Owls, and orchids—of these forested peatlands before they are released for commercial exploitation.

Until recently, the tamarack forest was of only marginal value to forestry, occasionally being cut for fence posts or firewood. On this basis, in Manitoba we have had some tamarack stands set aside for Great Gray Owl nesting sites. Now, however, trees are being harvested in southeastern Manitoba for paper mills in Wisconsin. According to foresters, good regeneration of tamarack is obtained by clear-cutting, and this is the present practice. If commercial use of tamarack forests cannot be kept on a sustained-yield basis, this may be a threat to Great Gray Owl breeding habitat. This new demand for the tamarack resource is not limited to Manitoba, but wherever tamarack is abundant and accessible.

Some observers report that in recent years, as a result of extensive tree clearing and other forestry practices, owl habitat in Norway, Sweden, and Finland has greatly diminished. Human activities in formerly remote regions over much of its breeding range in North America pose an ever increasing threat through shooting and an equally deleterious effect on elimination of habitat. In west-central Alberta, local observers report that during the past fifty years thousands of acres of habitat suitable for, and probably occupied by breeding Great Gray Owls, have been destroyed by lumbering, closely followed by the clearing of land for agriculture. At present, so I am informed, this destruction is spreading into north-central Alberta. The same observers report that in central and west-central Alberta, where Great Gray Owls frequently appear in winter to forage in open meadows for voles and shrews, heavy use of the same site by skidoos is apparently causing a reduction in microtine use, or reduction of the populations of these small rodents. At the same time, Great Grays, and other owls, are visiting these areas less frequently. There are also reports of widespread destruction of habitat in western and northern Saskatchewan by mining exploration crews. In the Lac du Bonnet area, northeast of Winnipeg, important winter feeding grounds are rapidly being lost to cottage site development. According to biologist Jon Winter, loss of mature old-forest habitat within the Great Gray Owl's limited range in northern California has put this species on the endangered list for that state.

Despite these pessimistic aspects, there is still a lot of habitat for these adaptable owls. In our study area, for example, I am impressed with the amount of potential breeding habitat. As I stand on the crest of a sandy, morainal ridge that rises above the boglands of southeastern Manitoba, there is habitat as far as I can see. Out over the tops of birch, aspen, and jack pine on the near slopes, out over the black spruce and tamarack, a blue veil reaches to the horizon. Mile after mile of muskeg, hundreds of square miles of habitat—homes for owls. With this vista before me, it is easy to forget the overall, broader concerns for habitat loss. I wonder how we should ever know this region? How we should ever determine how many owls find haven here? How we should ever know where owls are now established, female on nest, male nearby?

Moreover, there are some additional interrelationships here and elsewhere that warrant study. Owls eat shrews; shrews eat pupating larch sawfly larvae; the larch sawfly kills or injures tamarack (larch) trees. The tamaracks we choose to build nests in may have been deformed as a result of larch sawfly attacks. Infestation by larch sawfly caused suppression and massive die-offs in the past, across the range of tamarack in the United States and Canada, followed by the invasion and dominance of black spruce. Larch sawfly is still a major threat to tamarack. This is an area of investigation with possible implications to Great Gray Owl distribution, past, present, and future.

Loggers, trappers, cross-country skiers, snowmobilers, many know these woods better than we do, especially in winter, but few follow our trail, which is an intellectual and emotional one, a tangle, a bog, a journey, and an exploration of its own. In how many moments have I pondered the difficulties of ever knowing anything about this bird, this owl that so resists our efforts? Watching for owls in the early dawn, looking at the jagged tops of spruce and tamarack against the orange rising sun, I have thought of the many unsolved problems, the seeming insurmountability of really ever knowing the essence of this bird.

It will be many years before there are enough banded birds even in the small area in which we are working for us to learn much about them. How to identify local resident birds from northern emigrants? How to distinguish family groups? How to census this portion of their breeding grounds? How can we estimate their total numbers, and how will we be able to measure their population changes from year to year? How can we know the extent to which emigrant birds help sustain local populations? Against the obvious heavy mortality that this species suffers, is it the occasional influx of more northerly birds that maintains their presence

here? How far do owls range in those winters when they appear suddenly in strange places, like strangers still wearing their native garb?

Clearly, in some winters Great Gray Owls must come from more northerly breeding ranges, for often winter appearances of Great Grays coincide with irruptions of Boreal Owls and Hawk Owls, neither of which appears to breed to any extent in southeastern Manitoba. Movements of Great Gray Owls into southern Minnesota, Wisconsin, Michigan, and southern Ontario further support this idea. How to determine which owls are local birds and which are emigrants is one of the major problems.

On a local basis, much insight has been gained into the distribution and movements of owls, but probably the solutions to many problems lie in the analysis of information from a much broader region. Across the whole range of the species, a host of climatic and ecological factors act upon these birds. Studies now in progress in California, Oregon, Minnesota, and Wisconsin should shed considerable light on these aspects.

Radio-telemetry and other technological marvels of this space-age era may yet yield answers to questions that have intrigued us for years. The distant signal of a radio-tagged owl winging through the forest on moonlit nights could lead us to a nest, carrying us over unknown reaches of bogland. The same technique could reveal the duration of the family bond and outline the movements of young and adults, long after the nest has been left behind.

One day, a student shivering in a tent near a nest site in mid-February may see the courtship ritual of the Great Gray Owl. On some frosty dawn, with the woods aglitter with the first light, he may see the graceful posturing and hear the soft calls, witness with fresh insight what we have barely glimpsed. It will be a tough, cold task, but one day we may know what the owls do at night, where they roost, how they go about in search of nests, and how they behave when looking over a potential nest site.

What manner of bird is this? What is the explanation for its tameness? "Tame" is probably a misnomer. Unwary, docile, unconcerned with man? And yet at times it attacks man violently. Still, its seeming docility is one of its most noted characteristics. Is this trait related to its usual range in remote northern areas far from man? Boreal, Saw-whet, and Hawk owls are equally docile. So too is the Spotted Owl, the Great Gray Owl's closest relative in North America; a southern subspecies of the Spotted Owl, nesting in New Mexico, is reportedly equally as bold or docile. Many birds are unusually bold at the nest site. Perhaps it is the large size of the Great Gray that makes this aspect of its behavior especially noticeable. The Great Gray Owl's response to man is, really, an unknown quality of the bird, a feature that adds to its attractiveness.

Years ago, Thoreau wrote: "I rejoice that there are owls. Let them do the idiotic and maniacal hooting for men. It is a sound admirably suited to swamps and twilight woods which no day illustrates, suggesting a vast and undeveloped nature which men have not recognized. They represent the stark twilight and unsatisfied thoughts which all have. All day the sun has shone on the surface of some savage swamp, where the single spruce stands hung with usnea lichens, and small hawks circulate above, and the chickadee lisps amid the evergreens, and the partridge and rabbit skulk beneath; but now a more dismal and fitting day dawns, and a different race of creatures awakes to express the meaning of Nature there." He could, with that sentiment, have been writing about the Great Gray Owl.

However much is learned, there is some comfort, I think, in believing that the ultimate quality of a species, its essence, rests not in data alone, but in some impression in our minds, some subjective

An unwavering, steady stare that focuses past the photographer.

aspect. We probably can never really know any other creature fully. Though we catalog its comings and goings, measure and photograph its performances, count its numbers, and write endlessly about it, still, the true character of this "different race of creatures" eludes us.

In my own pursuit of the owl, I crave further understanding of its relationship to the spruce-tamarack bog and all it contains. What holds meaning for the owl? Being part of the bog, it relates to this environment in ways we'll probably never know. There are many barriers between us, but here I would venture. The owl has superior vision and hearing, but what does it perceive in its surroundings? When an owl drops down onto a mouse, does it notice the orchid blooming beside its feet? Or does it have visions of a nest, hungry young, or its mate? We say "it stares blankly," but we don't know what its visual world embraces. It hears everything we hear and more, but in what way? In sky, forest, flowers, and birds, we humans see patterns of light and color, hear a medley of sounds, perceive various elements according to our individual insights, sharing some, but not all. But ah! if we could perceive the world of the owl, what strange sounds and beautiful forms we might enjoy!

Bibliography

Allen, Francis H. "The Great Gray Owl near Boston." *Auk* 21 (1904): 278.

American Ornithologists' Union. *Check-list of North American Birds.* 5th ed. Baltimore, Md., 1957.

Angell, Tony. *Owls.* Seattle: University of Washington Press, 1974.

Audubon, John James. *The Birds of America.* Vol. 1. 1840.

Baird, Spencer F., et al. *A History of North American Birds.* Vol. 3. Boston: Little, Brown & Co., 1905.

Barrows, Walter B. *Michigan Bird Life.* East Lansing: Special Bulletin, Michigan Agricultural College, 1912.

Bell, Gary P. "The Owl Invasion of Amherst Island, Ontario." *American Birds* 33 (1979): 245–46.

Bent, Arthur C. "Life Histories of North American Birds of Prey." *U.S. National Museum Bulletin* 170, part 2, pp. 213–20. Washington, D.C.: Smithsonian Institution, 1938.

Berggren, Valdemar, and Wahlstedt, Jens. "Lappugglans *Strix nebulosa* läten." [The sound repertoire of the Great Gray Owl *Strix nebulosa.*] *Vår Fågelvärld* 36 (1977): 243–49.

Bird, David M., and Wright, Jo. "Apparent Distraction Display by a Barred Owl." *Canadian Field-Naturalist* 91 (1977): 176–77.

Blair, Hugh M.S. "Studies of Less Familiar Birds. 119. Great Grey Owl." *British Birds* 55 (1962): 414–18.

Blanich, Jo. "Summer Record of Great Gray Owls in Aitkin County." *Loon* 47 (1975): 188–89.

Brown, Herman J. "Bandits of the Pine Barrens." *Minnesota Naturalist* 3 (1953) 33–38.

Brunton, Daniel F., and Pittaway, Ronald, Jr. "Observations of the Great Gray Owl on Winter Range." *Canadian Field-Naturalist* 85 (1971): 315–22.

Buckner, Charles H. "Populations and Ecological Relationships of Shrews in Tamarack Bogs of Southeastern Manitoba." *Journal of Mammalogy* 47 (1966): 181–94.

Burton, John A., ed. *Owls of the World, Their Evolution, Structure and Ecology.* [Especially section on Great Gray Owl by Heimo Mikkola.] New York: E.P. Dutton, 1973.

Butler, Douglas H. "Great Gray Owl from Fillmore County." *Loon* 51 (1979): 46–47.

Clark, Richard J. *A Field Study of the Short-eared Owl, Asio flammeus (Pontoppidan), in North America.* Wildlife Monographs No. 47, Washington, D.C.: The Wildlife Society, 1975.

Collins, K. Michael. "Aspects of the Biology of the Great Gray Owl." Master's thesis (in preparation), University of Manitoba, Winnipeg.

Craighead, John J., and Craighead, Francis C., Jr. *Hawks, Owls and Wildlife.* New York: Dover Publications, 1956.

Dement'ev, Georgii P., et al. *Birds of the Soviet Union.* Vol. 1, Jerusalem: Israel Program for Scientific Translations, 1966.

Derleth, August. "Country Calendar: Autumn." *Passenger Pigeon* 14 (1952): 106–9.

Dunstan, Thomas C., and Sample, Steve D. "Biology of Barred Owls in Minnesota." *Loon* 44: 111–15.

Earhart, Caroline M., and Johnson, Ned K. "Size Dimorphism and Food Habits of North American Owls." *Condor* 72 (1970): 251–64.

Eckert, Allan W. *The Owls of North America.* Garden City, N.Y.: Doubleday & Co., 1974.

Eckert, Kim. "Invasion of Great Gray and Boreal Owls, Winter 1977–78." *Loon* 50 (1978): 63–68.

Elton, Charles S. *Voles, Mice and Lemmings: Problems in Population Dynamics.* Oxford: Clarendon Press, 1942.

Everett, Michael. *A Natural History of Owls.* London: Hamlyn Publishing Group Limited, 1977.

Ferguson-Lees, I. James. "Photographic Studies of Some Less Familiar Birds. LXIX. Great Grey Owl." *British Birds* 49 (1956): 26–27.

Fisher, Bob M. "Response of a Hawk Owl to a Lure." *Blue Jay* 32 (1974): 154–55.

———. "Possible Intra-specific Killing by a Great Gray Owl." *Canadian Field-Naturalist* 89 (1975): 71–72.

Fitzpatrick, John W. "A Record of Allopreening in the Barred Owl." *Auk* 92 (1975): 598–99.

Fleay, David. *Nightwatchmen of Bush and Plain.* [Australian Owls and Owl-like Birds.] Brisbane: The Jacaranda Press, 1968.

Follen, Don G., Sr. "A Probable Breeding Record of Great Gray Owls in Wisconsin." *Passenger Pigeon* 41 (1979): 53–57.

Forbush, Edward H. *Birds of Massachusetts and Other New England States.* Vol. 2. Norwood: Massachusetts Department of Agriculture, 1927.

Forsman, Eric D., and Wight, Howard M. "Allowpreening in Owls: What Are Its Functions?" *Auk* 96 (1979): 525–31.

Forster, John R. "An Account of the Birds Sent from Hudson's Bay." *Transactions of the Philadelphia Royal Society,* vol. 62. pp. 382–433. Philadelphia, 1772.

Godfrey, W. Earl. "The Birds of Canada." *National Museum of Canada Bulletin* 203. Ottawa, 1966.

———. "Some Winter Aspects of the Great Gray Owl." *Canadian Field-Naturalist* 81 (1967): 99–101.

Green, Janet C. "Northern Owl Invasion, Winter, 1968–1969." *Loon* 41 (1969): 36–39.

Grey Owl [Archie, Belaney]. *Pilgrims of the Wild.* London: Peter Davies, 1939.

Hausman, Leon A. *The Illustrated Encyclopedia of American Birds.* New York: Garden City Publishing Co., 1947.

Henderson, Archibald D. "Nesting of the Great Gray Owl in Central Alberta." *Oölogist* 32 (1915): 2–6.

———. "Further Notes on the Nesting of the Great Gray Owl." *Oölogist* 40 (1923): 126–27.

Höglund, Nils H., and Lansgren, Erik. "The Great Grey Owl and Its Prey in Sweden." *Viltrevy* 5 (1968): 363–421.

Houston, [C.] Stuart. "The Great Gray Owl in Saskatchewan." *Blue Jay* 15 (1959): 150–53.

Houston, C. Stuart. "Reproduction in Great Horned Owls." *Bird Banding* 46 (1975): 302–4.

———. "Recoveries of Saskatchewan-banded Great Horned Owls." *Canadian Field Naturalist* 92 (1978): 61–66.

Houston, C. Stuart, and Street, Maurice. *The Birds of the Saskatchewan River, Carlton to Cumberland.* Special Publication no. 2, Saskatchewan Natural History Society, Regina.

Irving, Laurence. "Birds of Anaktuvak Pass, Kobruk, and Old Crow." *U.S. National Museum Bulletin* 217. Washington, D.C.: Smithsonian Institution, 1959.

James, Ross D. "First Nesting of the Great Gray Owl in Ontario." *Ontario Field Biologist* 31 (1977): 55.

Jenness, Diamond. "The Ojibwa Indians of Parry Island, Their Social and Religious Life." *National Museum of Canada Bulletin* 78. Ottawa, 1935.

Jones, Edgar T. "The Great Gray Owl." *Blue Jay* 12 (1954): 8.

Konishi, Masakazu. "How the Owl Tracks Its Prey." *American Scientist* 61 (1973): 414–24.

Kondla, Norbert G. "Great Gray Owls Raise Two Young Southeast of Edmonton, Alberta." *Blue Jay* 31 (1973): 98–100.

Lambert, Gordon. "A New Species is Added to North American Bird Life." *Bird-Banding* 18 (1947): 129–30.

Law, Clifford. "The Great Gray Owl of the Woodlands." *Blue Jay* 18 (1960): 14–16.

Leopold, Aldo. *Round River.* New York: Oxford University Press, 1953.

Lindblad, Jan. *I ugglemarker.* [Owl-watcher.] Stockholm: Alb. Bonniers boktrykeri, 1967.

McKay, William E. "The Great Grey Owl." *Dinny's Digest* [Calgary Zoo.] 2 (1972): 16, 18.

McKeever, Katherine. *Care and Rehabilitation of Injured Owls.* The Owl Rehabilitation Research Foundation, Vineland, Ontario. Lincoln, Ont.: Rannie, 1979.

Macoun, John. *Catalogue of Canadian Birds.* Part 2. Ottawa: Geological Survey of Canada, 1903.

Madura, Marilu L. "Feathered Observations." *Passenger Pigeon* 14 (1952): 99–102.

Mikkola, Heimo. "Food of Great Grey Owls in Fenno-Scandia." *British Birds* 63 (1970): 23–27.

———. "Lapinpöllöjen joukkokuolema vuonna 1971." [Population crash of the Great Gray Owl in Finland in 1971.] *Suomen Luonto* 30 (1971): 177–79, 213.

———. "Owls Killing and Killed by Other Owls and Raptors in Europe." *British Birds* 69 (1976): 144–54.

———. *Der Bartkauz* |Great Gray Owl.| A Ziemsen Verlag, Witt. L., Neue Brehm-Bücherei no. 51, 1981.

Mikkola, Heimo, and Sulkava, Seppo. "On the Occurrence of the Great Gray Owl *(Strix nebulosa)* in Finland 1955–68." *Ornis Fennica* 46 (1969): 126–31.

Mitchell, Bob. "The Great Gray Owl." *Wildlife Crusader* 15 (1969): 24–25.

Molhoff, Wayne J. "Great Gray Owl Distribution, Winter 1977–78." *Nebraska Bird Review* 47 (1979): 62–65.

Muir, Dalton. "At a Nest of the Great Gray Owl." *Nature Canada* 1 (1972): 20–22.

Nero, Robert W. "The Status of the Great Gray Owl in Manitoba, with Special Reference to the 1968–69 Influx." *Blue Jay* 27 (1969): 191–209.

———. "Great Gray Owls Nesting Near Roseau." *Loon* 42 (1970a): 88–93.

———. "A Visit to a Great Gray Owl Nest." *Ontario Naturalist* 8 (1970b): 4–7.

———. "Additional Great Gray Owl Records for Manitoba and Adjacent Minnesota." *Blue Jay* 28 (1970c): 72–73.

———. "Spirit of the Boreal Forest: the Great Gray Owl." *Beaver* 302 (1971): 25–29.

———. "Great Gray Owl Impaled on Barbed Wire." *Blue Jay* 32 (1974): 178–79.

———. "Great Gray Owl Nests." *Manitoba Nature* 17 (1977a): 4–11.

————. "Great Gray Owls in Our Woods." *Wildlife Crusader* 23 (1977b): 10–12.

————. "Beware: Mother on Nest." *International Wildlife* 8 (1978): 12–15.

Nero, Robert W., et al. "Great Gray Owls Occupy Artificial Nest." *Loon* 46 (1974): 161–65.

Norman, Ernest S. "Additions to the Birds of Shoal Lake, Manitoba." *Canadian Field-Naturalist* 34 (1920): 154.

Nuttall, Thomas. "The Land Birds." In *A Manual of the Ornithology of the United States and Canada.* 2nd ed. Cambridge: Hilliard & Brown, 1840.

Oeming, Albert F. "In Quest of the Rare Great Gray Owl." *Canadian Geographical Journal* 73 (1955): 236–43.

————. "The Great Grey Owl." *Game Bird Breeders, Pheasant Fanciers and Aviculturists' Gazette,* August 1970.

————. *A Preliminary Study of the Great Gray Owl (Scotiaptex nebulosa nebulosa) (Forster) in Alberta with Observations on Some Other Species of Owls.* Master's thesis, University of Alberta, Edmonton, 1955.

Parmelee, David F. "Nesting of the Great Gray Owl in Manitoba." *Blue Jay* 26 (1968): 120–21.

————. "Canada's Incredible Arctic Owls." *Beaver* 303 (1972): 30–41.

Payne, Roger S. "How the Barn Owl Locates Its Prey." *The Living Bird* (1962): 151–89.

————. "Acoustic Location of Prey by Barn Owls (*Tyto alba*)." *Journal of Experimental Biology* 54 (1971): 535–73.

Pearson, T. Gilbert, ed. *Birds of America.* New York: Garden City Publishing Co., 1917.

Peck, George K. "Recent Revision to the List of Ontario's Breeding Birds." *Ontario Field Biologist* 30 (1976): 9–16.

Pittaway, Ronald, Jr., and Brunton, Daniel. "The Great Gray Owl—Fact and Fiction." *Trail & Landscape* 3 (1969): 94–97.

Pulliainen, Erkki, and Loisa, Kalevi. "Breeding Biology and Food of the Great Grey Owl, *Strix nebulosa,* in Northeastern Finnish Forest Lapland." *Aquilo Ser. Zoology* 17 (1977): 23–33.

Richardson, John, and Swainson, William. *Fauna Boreali-Americana.* Vol. 2. The Birds. London: John Murray, 1831.

Roberts, Thomas S. *The Birds of Minnesota.* Vol. 2. Minneapolis: University of Minnesota Press, 1932.

————. "Great Gray Owl, *Scotiaptex nebulosa nebulosa,* Nesting in Minnesota." *Journal of Minnesota Ornithology* 1 (1936): 65–66.

Robinson, Ed. "Found Nest of the Great Gray Owl." *Blue Jay* 12 (1954): 20.

Salt, W. Ray, and Salt, James R. *The Birds of Alberta, with Their Ranges in Saskatchewan and Manitoba.* Edmonton: Hurtig Publishers, 1976.

Saurola, P. "Artificial Nest Construction in Europe." In *Bird of Prey Management Techniques.* Edited by T. A. Geer. British Falconers' Club, 1978.

Sept, Duane. "Great Gray Owl and Whip-poor-will in Prince Albert National Park." *Blue Jay* 34 (1976): 164–65.

Smith, F. Napier. "The American Hawk Owl (*Surnis* [sic] *ulula caparoch*)." *Canadian Field-Naturalist* 36 (1922): 68–71.

Sparks, John, and Soper, Tony. *Owls, Their Natural and Unnatural History.* New York: Taplinger Publishing Co., 1970.

Stefansson, Ove. "Lappuggla (*Strix nebulosa*) i Norrbotten 1975–1978." *Norrbottens Natur* 34 (1978): 49–63.

Stewart, Robert E., et al. "Live Trapping of Hawks and Owls." *Journal of Wildlife Management* 9 (1945): 99–105.

Taverner, Percy A. "Great Gray Owl." (In General Notes.) *Auk* 29 (1912): 397.

Taylor, Philip S. "Breeding Behavior of the Snowy Owl." *The Living Bird, Twelfth Annual* (1973): 137–53.

Thompson, Ernest E. [Ernest Thompson Seton.] "The Birds of Manitoba." *Proceedings of the U.S. National Museum* [*Smithsonian Institution*], vol. 13, pp. 457–643. Washington, D.C., 1891.

Thoreau, Henry David. *Walden*. New York: New American Library of World Literature, 1942.

Todd, W.E. Clyde. *Birds of the Labrador Peninsula and Adjacent Areas*. Toronto: University of Toronto Press, 1963.

Tucker, James A. "ABA's 50 Most Wanted Birds." *Birding* 4 (1972): 189–90.

Turnock, William J. "Ecological Life-History of the Larch Sawfly, *Pristiphora erichsonii* (HTG.) (Hymenoptera: Tenthredinidae), in Manitoba and Saskatchewan." *Canadian Entomologist* 92 (1960): 500–516.

Tyler, Hamilton, and Phillips, Don. *Owls by Day and Night*. Naturegraph Books: 987 Happy Camp, Calif., 1977.

Vickery, Peter D., and Yunick, Robert P. "The 1978–1979 Great Gray Owl Incursion Across Northeastern North America." *American Birds* 33 (1979): 242–44.

Wahlstedt, Jens. "Jakt, matning och läten hos lappuggla *Strix nebulosa*." [Hunting, Feeding, and Vocalization of the Great Gray Owl.] *Vår Fågelvärld* 28 (1969): 89–101.

———. "Lappugglan *Strix nebulosa* i Sverige 1973." [The Great Gray Owl in Sweden in 1973.] *Vår Fågelvärld* 33 (1974): 132–39.

———. "Lappugglan *Strix nebulosa* i Sverige 1974." [The Great Gray Owl in Sweden in 1974.] *Vår Fågelvärld* 35 (1976): 122–25.

Walker, Lewis W. *The Book of Owls*. [Especially section on Great Gray Owls by Albert F. Oeming.] New York: A.A. Knopf, 1974.

Wechsler, Charles A. "Gray Ghost of the Boreal Forest." *Minnesota Volunteer* 36 (1973): 25–30.

Williams, Glyndwr, and Glover, Richard, eds. *Andrew Grahman's Observations on Hudson's Bay 1767–91*. The Hudson's Bay Record Society, London, 1969.

Index

Alaska, 59, 82, 87, 96, 151
Alberta, 32, 35, 59, 62, 65, 86, 95, 98, 103,
 151
  government of, 68
Allen, Francis H., 32
Alymer (Quebec), 28
American Birding Association, 29
American Robin, 15
Amherst Island (Ontario), 28, 63
Arctic Circle, 35
Audubon, John James, 86

Bailey, Vernon, 51
Bal-chatri, 46, 51, 104
Barn Owl, 88
Barrows, Walter B., 97
Barred Owl, 29, 83, 84, 107
Belvedere (Alberta), 65
Bent, Arthur C., 72, 87
Berggren, Valdemar, 83
Bird, David M., 84
Black bear, 95
Black-capped Chickadee, 37, 122
Blue Jay, 15, 122, 126
Boreal Chickadee, 28
Boreal chorus frog, 16
Boreal Owl, 24, 29, 68, 92, 96, 153
British Columbia, 59
Broad-winged Hawk 102, 128, 145
Brown, Herman J., 99
Brunton, Daniel F., 28, 48, 83, 88, 90, 93
Butler, Douglas, 63

California, 59, 151, 153
Canada, 59, 62, 98
Caribou, 57
Carlson, Elsie, 44
Churchill (Manitoba), 96
Collins, K. Michael, 12, 126
Common Crow, 32, 59, 95, 102
Common Flicker, 15, 122
Common Goldeneye, 16
Common Raven, 24, 59, 95, 102
Common Snipe, 146
Connecticut Warbler, 126
Copland, Herbert W.R., 12, 38, 42, 45, 54,
 63, 92, 115, 128, 139

Cotter, George, 96
Cradle boards, 96
Craighead, Francis C., Jr., 95, 103
Craighead, John J., 95, 103

Dall, William H., 83, 87
Dedham (Massachusetts), 29
de Graff, Ken, 110
Dirks, Henry T., M.D., 114
Donald, John, 56
Dragonfly, 87
Duluth (Minnesota), 29, 64

Eastman, Karen, 131
Edmonton (Alberta), 32, 35
Elton, Charles S., 63
Eurasia, 58
Europe, 62

Field, James Thomas, 39
Finland, 59, 77, 86, 151
Fisher, Bob, 48, 86
Fitzpatrick, John W., 107
Forbush, Edward H., 63
Forest tent caterpillar, 126
Forsman, Eric D., 108
Forster, John R., 58, 72
Fort Severn (Ontario), 58
Fryklund, Per O., 114
Fur trade era, 58

Gill (Massachusetts), 29
Godfrey, W. Earl, 86, 88, 90
Golden Eagle, 35, 95
Goshawk, 15, 16, 65, 80, 95, 99
Graham, Andrew, 58, 73, 88
Grand Rapids (Manitoba), 96
Gray Jay, 24, 28, 33, 122, 126, 142
Great Bear Lake, 58, 62
Great Gray Owl (Strix nebulosa)
  acoustical ability, 73, 87, 88
  agonistic display, 77, 105
  allopreening (mutual preening), 107–9
  apteria, 82
  banding, 23, 45, 56
  band recoveries, 63
  bathing, 17

behavior, 48–49
bill color, 76
bill snapping, 41, 58, 77, 128, 130
breeding grounds, 24, 32
brood patch, 111, 114
capture techniques, 45–56
capturing a female, 130–31, 134
capturing an owl, 39
carrion feeding, 86–87
caught on barbed wire, 44
chick, accidental loss of, 124–25
clutch size, 102
collision with motor vehicles, 98
common names, Eurasian and North
    American, 58
concealment behavior, 80
conservation of, 99
cooling methods, 82
copulation, 84, 110
courtship, 102–4
courtship feeding, 66, 67, 101–4, 109–10
density, 62
description of, 33, 59, 72, 73, 76–83
differences in sexes, 72
distraction display (injury feigning), 36,
    84, 122, 130–31
effects of capture, 56
effects of weather, 45, 93
egg shape and size, 102–3
electrocuted, 98
Eurasian race: S.n. lapponica, 58
feather traits, 82
feeding behavior, 117, 120
female aggressiveness, 56, 121, 122, 131
female attentiveness, 120
female behavior, 117–18
female boldness at nest, 126
female luring young from nest site, 127
female stealing prey from male, 120–21
first banded, 45
fledging behavior, 118
fledglings, 118, 122
food habits, 86, 87
flight ability, 34–35
growth rate, 102
gunning mortality, 97, 98
habitat, 59
hatching, 117
harassment by Common Crow, 95

incubation, 111–12
irruptions (incursions), 63, 86, 98, 108
length of family bond, 122
looking for natural nests, 149–50
loss of young from nest, 118
male feeds female, 17
male hunting behavior, 127–28
man-made nests, use of, 139, 142, 145,
    146
marking techniques, 45,
molt, 73
mortality by man, 95–96,
museum specimens, 21
nest at The Pas (Manitoba), 16–17
nest building, 102
nest desertion, 125
nest, first in Minnesota, 114
nest, second in Minnesota, 114–22
nest, first known to science, 58
nests, Alberta, 65, 68
nests, man-made, 106, 139, 145, 147,
    153
nests, number of, 59, 62, 65, 68
nests, early visits to, 138, 142, 145
nesting behavior, 138
nests, other, 125–34
nest site, 102
nest site selection, 103
nictitating membrane, 41, 143
nomadic habits, 62–63, 86
North American race: S.n. nebulosa, 58
number banded, 45
oil gland, 81
owl nest search behavior, 145
pair formation, 102, 103–106
peat mining, 151
pellets, 40, 118
perching on wires, 33
periods of activity, 93
plumage characteristics, 72–73, 76
population, 21, 24, 45, 59, 62–63, 64,
    65
predation on, 95
preening behavior, 17, 81
preening response to man, 41, 106–7
pre-fledging behavior, 118
prey, 62, 86, 87
protective coloration, 80
pseudo-hunting behavior, 104–5

range, 59–65
taking prey from man, 120, 121
rehabilitation of owls, 100
relationship to prey, 102
repeat use of nests, 62–63
response of captured bird, 66
response to man-made lure, 48, 49
Saskatchewan records of, 65
scientific collecting, 62
scientific names, 58
sexual behavior, 103–4, 110
snow plunging (to capture prey; in
    courtship), 88–93
subspecies, Eurasian, 58
subspecies, North American, 58
sun bathing, 81
specimens of, 58, 98–99
talons, 81
territorial behavior, 103, 106
territory (range) size, 103
trapping mortality, 96–98
twig nibbling, 145–46
use by Indians, 96
use of a wing for balance when
    perched, 34
visits to nests by birds, 110–11, 146,
    149, 150
visual acuity, 92–93
vocalizations, 40, 69, 83–84, 103, 122,
    126–27, 128
weights, 58, 72
winter concentration, Minnesota, 114
winter irruptions, 63–64, 65
Great Horned Owl, 24, 29, 35, 65, 69, 72,
    95, 96, 97–98, 139, 145
Green, Janet C., 98

Halvorson, Henry, 114
Harrier (Marsh Hawk), 127
Hawk Owl, 24, 29, 48, 68, 92, 120, 153
Henderson, Archibald D., 32, 65, 97, 103,
    125
Herbert, Jack D., 16
Herchmer (Manitoba), 96
Hoary bat, 145
Höglund, Nils H., 102, 103, 118, 121, 122
House Sparrow, 42, 46
Houston, C. Stuart, M.D., 65
Hudson Bay, 58, 73, 96

Idaho, 59
Irving, Laurence, 96

James Bay, 59, 95
Jenness, Diamond, 96
Jones, Edgar T., 68
Jyrkkanen, Jorma, 40

Kingston (Ontario), 29, 63
Knapton, Richard W., 92
Kondla, Norbert G., 32

Lac du Bonnet (Manitoba), 34, 95
Lake of the Woods, 21
Lake Superior, 58
Lambert, Gordon, 45
Lambeth, David, 33
Lansgren, Erik, 102, 103, 104, 106, 108
Larch sawfly, 153
Law, Clifford, 77, 88
Lawrence, Alex G., 41, 42, 95
Least Flycatcher, 126
Leinonen, Antti, 95
Leopold, Aldo, 150
Lincoln's Sparrow, 131
Loisa, Kaleni, 77
Long-eared Owl, 77, 145
Lynx, 57, 94, 96

McKay, William E., 98
McKeever, Katherine, 100, 108
Madura, Marilu L., 47
Maine, 98
Mallard, 95, 99
Manitoba, 16, 21, 45, 58, 62, 64, 82, 86,
    95, 100
    Department of Natural Resources, 98
    Hydro-Electric of, 98
Marblehead (Massachusetts), 86
Marten, 34, 86–87
Maryland, 29
Massachusetts, 86, 98
Meadow vole, 46, 48, 50, 90, 117, 118
Michigan, 97, 153
Mikkola, Heimo, 59, 86, 95
Minnesota, 21, 59, 62, 98, 114, 124, 128,
    151, 153
Mistletoe, 32
Montana, 59

Montreal (Quebec), 32, 98
Montreal Island (Quebec), 98
Moose, 24
Moose Factory (Ontario), 95, 96
Moosonee (Ontario), 24, 34, 86
Mossop, Harold, 39, 98
Mourning Warbler, 130
Muir, Dalton, 12, 35, 115, 116, 117

New England States, 63, 64
New Jersey, 29
New York, 63, 64
Newell, Charles E., 131
Nordstrom, Clarence, 114
Norman, Ernest S., 82
North America, 58, 59, 62
North Dakota, 33
Norway, 58, 151
Norway rat, 87
Nulato (Alaska), 87
Nuttall, Thomas, 86, 88

Oeming, Albert F., 35, 49, 65, 77, 95, 97,
    107
Ontario, 29, 58, 59, 64, 96, 100, 153
Oregon, 153
Ottawa, 48, 63, 83, 108, 120
Ovenbird, 126
Owl Rehabilitation Research
    Foundation, 100, 108

Parmelee, David F., 16, 84, 102
Parry Sound (Ontario), 96
Peat, commercial use of, 151
Pileated Woodpecker, 16
Pine Grosbeak, 28
Pittaway, Ronald, 29, 48, 88, 93
Porcupine, 145
Poulin, Richard M., 108
Precambrian Shield, 21
Pulliainen, Erkki, 77

Quebec, 29, 59, 64, 98

Radio-telemetry, 153
Reader, Philip B., 16, 17
Red-backed vole, 70, 85, 91
Redpoll, 87
Red squirrel, 46, 87, 97, 139, 149

Red-tailed Hawk, 20, 32, 47, 65, 77, 102,
    130, 139, 145
Red-winged Blackbird, 146
Rehabilitation of raptors, 100
Richardson, Sir John, 58, 62, 72
Riveredge Foundation, 39
Rhode Island, 72
Roberts, Thomas S., 87
Robertson, Ed, 16
Rocky Mountain House (Alberta), 98
Rose-breasted Grosbeak, 126
Royal Canadian Mounted Police, 24, 25
Ruffed Grouse, 15, 94, 96, 99

St. Lawrence River, 29, 32
Sandhill Crane, 146, 150
Saskatchewan, 59, 65, 77
Sault Ste. Marie (Michigan), 97
Saw-whet Owl, 29, 153
Scandinavia, 86, 102, 138
Scientific permits, 45
Sealy, Spencer G., 12, 124, 125, 126, 127,
    139
Severn (Ontario), 88
Severn River (Ontario), 58
Sharp-tailed Grouse, 87
Shortt, Angus H., 29, 40
Short-tailed shrew, 46
Siberia, 59
Smith, F. Napier, 32, 120
Snowshoe hare, 15, 57, 65, 86, 95
Snowy Owl, 72, 83, 84, 96, 102
Song Sparrow, 130
Soviet Union, 58
Spotted Owl, 108, 153
Steel trap, 96–97
Stitt, Robert, 24, 34, 86
Street, Maurice, 86
Swainson, William, 58
Swainson's Thrush, 126
Swastika (Ontario), 98
Sweden, 35, 58, 63, 103, 110, 118, 122,
    138, 151

Tamarack, commercial use of, 151
Taylor, Philip S., 102
Taylor, Robert R., 12, 16, 20, 25, 42, 81,
    87, 114, 121, 124, 126
Texas, 29

The Pas (Manitoba), 16, 33, 56
Thoreau, Henry David, 153
Todd, W.E. Clyde, 95, 96
Toronto (Ontario), 45
Tuokko, Raymond, 12, 95, 104, 106, 145

United States, 29, 62
Verbail trap, 51
Verdun (Quebec), 32
Vineland (Ontario), 100, 108

Wabowden (Manitoba), 110
Wahlberg, Kapten, 35
Wahlstedt, Jens, 34, 63, 77, 83–84, 118,
    122
Waller, Sam, 96
Wight, Howard M., 108
Whistling Swan, 20
White-throated Sparrow, 126
White-winged Crossbill, 142
Wickford (Rhode Island), 72
Winisk (Ontario), 96
Winnipeg, 16, 21, 29, 38, 39, 63, 64, 92,
    98, 106, 114, 121, 124, 142
  Hydro-Electric of, 98
Winter Wren, 126, 131
Wisconsin, 59, 150, 151, 153
Witches'-broom, 32
Wood frog, 20
Wright, Jo, 84
Wyoming, 59, 103

Yukon River (Alaska), 82